NAFTA AT 20

NAFTA
AT 20

The North American
Free Trade Agreement's
Achievements and Challenges

Edited by
Michael J. Boskin

HOOVER INSTITUTION PRESS
Stanford University | *Stanford, California*

The Hoover Institution on War, Revolution and Peace, founded at Stanford University in 1919 by Herbert Hoover, who went on to become the thirty-first president of the United States, is an interdisciplinary research center for advanced study on domestic and international affairs. The views expressed in its publications are entirely those of the authors and do not necessarily reflect the views of the staff, officers, or Board of Overseers of the Hoover Institution.

www.hoover.org

Hoover Institution Press Publication No. 655

Hoover Institution at Leland Stanford Junior University,
Stanford, California 94305-6010

First printing 2014
20 19 18 17 16 15 14   7 6 5 4 3 2

Manufactured in the United States of America

The paper used in this publication meets the minimum Requirements of the American National Standard for Information Sciences—Permanence of Paper for Printed Library Materials, ANSI/NISO Z39.48-1992. ⊗

Cataloging-in-Publication Data is available from the Library of Congress.

ISBN: 978-0-8179-1814-9 (cloth. : alk. paper)
ISBN: 978-0-8179-1815-6 (pbk. : alk. paper)
ISBN: 978-0-8179-1816-3 (epub)
ISBN: 978-0-8179-1817-0 (mobi)
ISBN: 978-0-8179-1818-7 (PDF)

Contents

Abbreviations

AFORES	Administradora de Fondos para el Retiro
APEC	Asia-Pacific Economic Cooperation
CAFE	corporate average fuel economy
CAFTA	Central American Free Trade Agreement
CUSFTA	Canada-US Free Trade Agreement
EPA	Environmental Protection Agency
FDI	foreign direct investment
FTA	free trade agreement
GATT	General Agreement on Tariffs and Trade
GDP	gross domestic product
GSP	Generalized System of Preferences
ITAC	International Trade Advisory Committee
LNG	liquefied natural gas
MFN	most favored nation
NAFTA	North American Free Trade Agreement
OECD	Organisation for Economic Co-operation and Development
OPEC	Organization of the Petroleum Exporting Countries
PAN	Partido Acción Nacional, or National Action Party
PRD	Partido de la Revolución Democrática, or Party of the Democratic Revolution
PRI	Partido Revolucionario Institucional, or Institutional Revolutionary Party
SAFTA	South Asian Free Trade Area
SAGIT	Sectoral Advisory Group on International Trade
SEC	Securities and Exchange Commission
SITC	Standard International Trade Classification
TPP	Trans-Pacific Partnership
TTIP	Transatlantic Trade and Investment Partnership
USTR	United States Trade Representative
WTO	World Trade Organization

List of Figures and Tables

Table

Preface

The North American Free Trade Agreement—NAFTA—was signed in late 1992, passed by Congress in mid-1993, and initiated on January 1, 1994. On December 9, 2013, the Hoover Institution of Stanford University hosted a conference on **NAFTA at Twenty: The Past, Present, and Future of the North American Free Trade Agrecment**. Its goal was to bring together distinguished academics who had studied the effects of NAFTA with high-level policymakers, most importantly those who actually negotiated the treaty. The idea was to get the "NAFTA story" in one place, from the perspective of economists, historians, and policymakers, in easily accessible, non-technical summaries in the words of those undertaking the negotiating and research. This volume is the result of the conference, which was also streamed live on the Internet, with podcasts of the different presentations available on the Hoover Institution website, http://www.hoover.org/news/175776.

The volume should be of interest not only to students and scholars in economics, history, international relations, and political science more broadly, but also to those seeking to learn lessons from the NAFTA story applicable to other trade pacts, for these or other countries, current or prospective.

NAFTA was bold, innovative, risky, and controversial from the start. It became a political lightning rod and poster child for complaints about globalization, growth, the decline of organized labor, and capitalism. And it became the template for hundreds of subsequent free trade agreements.

In the Introduction, I briefly discuss the economic and trade policy environment in the time running up to the idea of launching negotiations on a free trade agreement between the United States and Mexico, which soon evolved into the trilateral NAFTA. It was by no means clear that it could be successfully negotiated as a broad free trade agreement, given various domestic economic interests in each country, even less while the Uruguay Round of the General Agreement on Tariffs and Trade was on the table. But successfully negotiated and passed by Congress it was, in considerable measure because of the talent and effort of the negotiators and their backing by the respective heads of government. And the net benefits to the three nations have been substantial.

In chapter 1, the three main negotiators, Jaime Serra Puche of Mexico, Carla Hills of the United States, and Michael Wilson of Canada, describe NAFTA's origins from how the idea was born to the goals for it, well beyond trade, of the elected leaders. Wilson discusses the economic and political origins and passage of the Canada-US Free Trade Agreement which preceded NAFTA. Like NAFTA, CUSFTA was controversial, especially in Canada. The Canadians sought not only the traditional benefits from trade, but also a tool for modernizing the Canadian economy, making it more competitive. Jaime Serra Puche describes the economic and political context which led Mexican president Carlos Salinas de Gortari to have him raise the subject of a free trade agreement (FTA) with Hills in a meeting previously scheduled to discuss a narrower trade issue. Hills describes the process by which she was able to bring a recalcitrant US Congress along during the negotiations. All three, joined by Mickey Kantor, describe the give and take in the negotiations, the extensive consultation with business and labor groups in their respective countries, and the complex navigation of US congressional approval.

In chapter 2, Stephen Haber describes the economic and political equilibrium in Mexico before and after NAFTA, attributing the remarkable improvement in the economy and dramatic democratization of Mexico primarily to the effects of NAFTA. Prior to NAFTA, the Mexican economy and polity were closed and monopolized. After, and to a considerable extent because of NAFTA, the Mexican economy and political process became far more competitive. Daniel Trefler performs a similar analysis of the Canadian economy, focusing on the tremendous improvements in productivity of Canadian firms brought about by CUSFTA and NAFTA. The gains are remarkable, amounting to a decade's worth of improvements in living standards from the various ways in which Canadian firms and their workers adapted following the trade agreements.

Chapter 3 is the luncheon address by George Shultz, describing the fundamental transformation of North America, both economically and politically. He believes that North America has arrived as a potent force on the global scene, well in excess of the considerable individual importance of the three countries. This is driven by the integration of the three economies, including a substantial processing supply chain that, to take one example, now has 40 percent of Mexico's exports to the United States as re-exported US content originally imported to Mexico at an earlier stage of production. The supply chain complementarity is matched by important complementarities in demography and energy which have the potential to increase still more the prosperity and security of the three nations. Perhaps most importantly, Mexico increasingly thinks of itself, and Canada and the United States think of Mexico, as part of a North American identity, not merely geography. To be sure, considerable problems as well as opportunities remain. Shultz believes a much greater focus on the southern border of Mexico would pay the biggest dividends.

In chapter 4, Lorenzo Caliendo of Yale summarizes his econometric research on the trade, real wage, and welfare gains which NAFTA has produced for each of the three countries. He pays particular attention to the inter-industry and intra-industry linkages and concludes that trade has soared and real wages risen for all three countries. But, of course, the gains were largest for the smallest economy, Mexico, which benefited by gaining access to the largest country and from initially having the largest tariffs. Caroline Freund summarizes her research on one of the vital questions surrounding bilateral or regional free trade agreements: do they merely expand trade among the participants by diverting it from other countries? Or is there a net expansion of trade and, if so, how much? By comparing the details of effective tariffs in different sectors for different products under the old and new regimes, she is able convincingly to conclude that diversion has been small, and trade expansion large under NAFTA.

In chapter 5, Jim Sweeney describes the major energy markets within and between the three countries. There is substantial integration between the United States and Canada, for example, in electricity. Canada exports virtually all of its oil to the United States, which imports oil from Mexico as well. Sweeney likewise examines coal, natural gas, etc., and explores the evolution of North America's net energy balance among the countries and between North America and the rest of the world. The shale oil and gas revolution and Canadian oil sands production have greatly tipped that balance in North America's favor, and Mexico is in the early stages of opening its declining oil industry to foreign investment and technology. Sweeney importantly notes that, because of the integration of the electricity markets (which greatly reduces price spikes and risks of brownouts and blackouts along with the need to build more power plants within each country), the welfare gain exceeds those from the actual trade. Michael Wilson discusses Canada's energy issues, opportunities, and likely evolution. He notes the shale revolution in the United States and its impact on Canada, and he persuasively argues that the additional two million barrels of oil a day that Canada can produce from its oil sands will be brought to market, whether sold to the United States, Europe, or Asia. The main roadblock is the long-delayed decision on the Keystone XL pipeline, which has become a major political as well as economic issue in Canada. He also presents a variety of other suggestions to take advantage of complementarity among the NAFTA partners.

In chapter 6, Serra Puche, Hills, and Wilson discuss the lessons from NAFTA for the future, both of NAFTA itself and of other trade agreements, including the Trans-Pacific Partnership (TPP) and Transatlantic Trade and Investment Partnership (TTIP), both currently in negotiations. They delve into the energy and labor mobility issues that NAFTA did not address and whether labor and environmental concerns are best dealt with in side agreements or as part of a treaty, opining on whether doing so would have made NAFTA impossible to enact. They also describe how these issues, plus complex rules of origin, can limit trade liberalization and/or reduce the benefits of existing agreements. Finally, they describe the fundamental importance of political leadership and provision of information on the benefits of trade liberalization to voters and potentially ill-informed politicians, who hear most loudly from the opponents.

The presentations in each chapter are followed by lively discussion among conference participants. The comments, questions, and answers help clarify, expand, and enrich the presentations and form an important part of the volume, as they did at the conference.

Michael J. Boskin
Stanford, California, 2014

Acknowledgments

A conference such as **NAFTA at Twenty** does not occur, let alone run smoothly, and a book such as this does not get into print without the diligence of many talented people. I owe a debt of gratitude to, and would like to acknowledge, all the participants in the conference, who approached their participation with seriousness and candor and among whom the discussion was spirited and insightful. That the people most responsible for NAFTA's negotiation and drafting, on the one hand, and its scholarly evaluation, on the other, could still learn from each other was more than ample recompense for my efforts in bringing them together. Special thanks go to Stanford Professor Kyle Bagwell, who at an early stage helped me think through the format and participants.

The support staff at Hoover covered everything from facilities to catering, from sound to Internet streaming and podcasts, to copyediting, all superbly, and certainly covered for me on numerous occasions. They included, in alphabetical order, Barbara Arellano, Sarah Bielecki, Marshall Blanchard, Barbara Egbert, Mary Gingell, Linda Hernandez, Katrina Kane, Jennifer Mayfield, Jim McCumsey, Jennifer Navarrette, Jennifer Presley, Ellen Santiago, Marie-Christine Slakey, Celeste Szeto, and Deborah Ventura. Economics graduate student Art Tosborvorn provided helpful support at several stages of the project.

My deepest debt of gratitude goes to my research and administrative assistants, Leilei Xu and Julia Ball, who made sure the conference and volume proceeded on schedule and, limited only by academic norms and budget, with style.

Introduction

Michael J. Boskin

The North American Free Trade Agreement (NAFTA) was bold and controversial from the start. As time passes, new events demand our attention, and we tend to take history and current institutions for granted. Thus, it is helpful to understand the economic and political situation in which NAFTA was conceived and negotiated. It was far from obvious that it would be possible under the circumstances.

There was a long recovery from the 1980 recession and the severe 1981–82 recession, which were byproducts of Fed Chairman Paul Volcker's disinflation. But the recovery was slowing dramatically in the United States and Canada at the end of the decade; Mexico had a difficult middle part of the decade but was improving. In particular, there had been the late 1987 stock market crash, which many thought would lead to another deep recession. The United States and Canada went into recession in 1990–1991. By historical standards, they were brief and mild, but anti-trade liberalization sentiment grows during difficult economic times.

There was a fierce US intellectual debate on free trade. Immense fear of Japan led to a clamor in some quarters, both in Congress and in the commentariat, to imitate many Japanese methods, to manage trade, to adopt more cartelized industrial organization structures, etc. Many Democrats—sometimes called Atari Democrats after the once-successful computer game company—were demanding managed trade, with the government picking technology winners and losers for subsidies via tax breaks, special spending, loans, and guarantees.

This terrible industrial policy idea has reemerged, unfortunately, in the last few years, both abroad and in the United States.

In the American system of government, presidents do not get to make economic decisions, including trade decisions, unilaterally. They have to go through Congress, which can be far more protectionist. It is important to note that even a staunch free trader like President Reagan wound up having to swallow auto and steel quotas.

Importantly, in the 1988 election, Vice President George H. W. Bush ran as a free trader. I can attest, from traveling on the campaign plane with him, that the constant attacks on his free trade position were intense. Michael Dukakis, the Democratic nominee, would hold his campaign rallies at plants which he claimed would soon be closed because of "unfair" trade.

If Bush had not believed in, and had not run on, free trade, even in textile-protectionist South Carolina, it would have been very difficult for him to get that far out ahead of the politics and public opinion when the time came to negotiate NAFTA.

The United States had the savings and loan crisis and the Third World debt problems of the money-center banks. Mexico had repudiated its debt in 1982, launching the Latin American debt crisis. Most major US money-center banks were insolvent, marking their debt to market. While the resulting tighter credit conditions were not nearly as severe as in the 2008–2009 financial crisis, these were considerable financial disruptions in their own right and were among the causes of the recession and modestly paced early recovery.

One of the first policies that the Bush administration implemented, to resolve the Latin American debt crisis, came to be called "Brady Bonds," after Treasury Secretary Nicholas Brady. The Federal Reserve was originally not supportive of writing down the bank debt. We had an internal debate about this and we went with the debt write-down. (By all accounts, it has been a success.) President Bush made it clear he wanted to do something to help Mexico, to strengthen our neighbor and our relations with it, and to aid the economic reformers in its government. That led me, with Secretary of State Jim Baker's backing, to suggest that, once the debt deal was done, we turn to trade liberalization with Mexico. As it turned out, the Mexican leadership was thinking along similar lines and proposed a full-blown free trade agreement that preempted our internal discussion.

The Canada-US Free Trade Agreement (CUSFTA) in 1987 was an important antecedent to NAFTA. There was some commentary post-CUSFTA on US-Mexico trade being next. Free trade agreements were rare at the time. There are hundreds of them now. We take them for granted, and it seems hard to think back to a time when they were rare. There was no major free trade agreement (FTA) between a large advanced economy and a developing economy, other than some arrangements with former colonies. And the multilateral global trade liberalization negotiation, the Uruguay Round of the General Agreement on Tariffs and Trade (GATT), was not firing on all cylinders at the time.

So the NAFTA idea was bold, novel, and risky. It ran against the intellectual current that trade liberalization ought to be done multilaterally. It was politically risky. No one could be certain what we could negotiate, what would come out of it, and what we could get Congress to pass. So putting ourselves back in that time to consider something we take for granted now is important.

Jaime Serra Puche and Carla Hills will describe their famous meeting in Davos, when the Mexican FTA proposal was first introduced. Secretary of State Jim Baker and I spent a couple of sessions championing it to President Bush in the Oval Office. Shortly after the Serra Puche-Hills Davos meeting, President Carlos Salinas de Gortari's chief of staff, Pepe Cordoba, came up to Washington. Baker and I met with him to discuss a US-Mexico FTA, which eventually became the trilateral NAFTA. Obviously, the leaders as well as their negotiators (including Commerce Secretary Robert Mosbacher) deserve a great deal of credit. At one point, we were concerned that Prime Minister Brian Mulroney's government would not survive the NAFTA proposal.

Mexico's tariffs were considerably higher than those of the United States or Canada and, of course, the United States is a much larger economy. So on balance, more was at stake for Mexico (and Canada, although the CUSFTA was already in force) than for the United States, as the other nations would be gaining greater access to a much larger market. There were great obstacles: protectionism, novelty, concerns over exporting US manufacturing jobs, fears of undermining GATT and of agricultural competition.

It is also important to note many concurrent events in the rest of the world. Deng Xiaoping's opening of China, Rajiv Gandhi's reforms in India, and the fall of the Berlin Wall were not only historically significant in their own right, they added over a billion potential workers to the global labor force. That was certain to place downward pressure on wages in the advanced economies. When combined with the development of new technology, this effect was reinforced. Hence NAFTA became a symbol of the downsides of these mostly positive developments and, for many years, took on blame out of any plausible proportion for any job or wage losses.

It is important to note that the result of NAFTA has been something far different from the simplistic outsourcing its opponents described. As Jaime Serra Puche notes later in this volume, NAFTA has " . . . transformed the region. We're not just selling things to each other; now we're producing things jointly." The United States imports large amounts of oil from Canada and Mexico, and did so well before NAFTA, which in any event has little influence on these oil flows. There is also sizable US content in exports to the US from Canada and Mexico (some, but less, vice versa). Netting out oil imports and adjusting for these re-exports, the United States is running a modest trade surplus on merchandise plus services with its NAFTA partners. A simple gravity-model analysis by my undergraduate honors student, Ed Zhu, reveals that NAFTA has increased trade among the United States, Canada, and Mexico by 84 percent, a larger impact than for any other major trade agreement.

To be clear, in any trade agreement the net benefits to the parties are composed of some losses as well as gains. For economic and humanitarian reasons, policies need to effectively ease the transition for the losers. But as sorting out the many effects of NAFTA from these factors and others has become possible, a clear picture emerges of the large net benefits NAFTA has generated and continues to generate.

There has also been something of an intellectual renaissance within economics in the field of international trade in the past dozen years. Scholars have developed new models and methods for understanding the nature of trade and measuring its gains in a complex global economy with many goods being traded among many nations. By and large, these studies suggest even larger potential gains from trade liberalization and, conversely, greater costs from protection, enhancing NAFTA's importance even more.

Chapter One

NAFTA: From Conception to Creation

The chief negotiators—Michael H. Wilson for Canada, Jaime Serra Puche for Mexico, and Carla A. Hills for the United States—reflect on the lengthy negotiations and political complications, interrupted by brief moments of drama, that culminated in the signing and ratification of the North American Free Trade Agreement.

Presenters: Michael H. Wilson, Jaime Serra Puche, Carla A. Hills, Mickey Kantor
Comments: George P. Shultz, Daniel Trefler, Michael J. Boskin

Michael H. Wilson: Let me put a little bit of historical context on all of this. Free trade with the United States had been a subject of discussion for probably a hundred years, on and off. We had another election, 1911, that was fought on free trade. The Liberals proposed it, Conservatives strongly opposed it, and the Conservatives won and that put the whole idea to bed for a long time because it was seen as a bit of a third rail.

We did take the first step in 1965 with the Auto Pact,[1] a very important trade agreement between the US and Canada. It was particularly important for Canada because it allowed us to modernize our sector. What happened out of that was about 90 percent of what we produced was sold in the United States, and about 90 percent of what we consumed was bought from the United States. So it was the first sign of real integration, and the start of the so-called North American Supply Chain.

---

1. Formally, the Canada-United States Automotive Products Agreement.

Then in the years leading up to the (Prime Minister Brian) Mulroney election in 1984, there was some talk of broadening from the Auto Pact and moving into other sectors. But it quickly became apparent that we would be taking the low-hanging fruit off the table and taking away the leverage that we would need to get a broader agreement on the much tougher issues that would become part of the overall agreement. The issue was not on the table at all in the 1984 election. The Liberal government had formed the Macdonald Commission, led by Don Macdonald, who is the foreign minister of everything in the Liberal government. He came up with a phrase which became the real talking point. He said that he thought that Canada should take a leap of faith and consider a free trade agreement with the United States.

Mulroney quickly grabbed this, and shortly after that we had the so-called Shamrock Summit in Quebec City with President Reagan and Prime Minister Mulroney agreeing to study the possibility of a free trade agreement between the two countries.

Throughout this period, President Reagan stood back from it. He did not want to be seen as being the aggressor taking the initiative. He very rightly thought that if he did that, it would attract a lot of negative attention in Canada, and he would become the focal point. He thought it would be better to have Mulroney take the initiative and the idea be seen as more of a Canadian idea, rather than something that the United States was imposing upon us.

But the underlying fear was that a free trade agreement with a country ten times the size of Canada both in terms of GDP and population would inevitably lead, directly or indirectly, to a significant erosion of our sovereignty. But in face of all of this, Mulroney, in September 1985, announced that he would propose a negotiation with the United States. President Reagan responded positively and enthusiastically.

Mulroney, though, in his announcement, was very careful to set out some of the things that he felt were the essence of Canada and would not be the subject of negotiation: our national sovereignty, our social policies, our cultural policies, the capacity to address regional disparities, our distinct linguistic character. These were the things that he focused on, understanding that these would become very significant in the concerns expressed by people opposed to the agreement.

But apart from that, he wanted the broadest package possible on the table. Inevitably, the cry went out right after that Mulroney was proposing to sell out Canada and that was something that carried through right into the subsequent election.

The key drivers in the negotiation were clear. We wanted to get access to a market ten times our size, our number one trading partner. We wanted to have access to the United States market because that would allow us to rationalize away from a very fragmented economy into an economy that was more integrated with this great big economy to our south, and allow us to specialize and focus on our areas of strength. These were very strong considerations.

Let me give you an example. I remember talking to a CEO of one of our large companies, and I said, "What would free trade do for you?" He said, "About a third of our business would be gone. Absolutely, we could not compete. Two-thirds would be OK."

I said, "One-third is quite a big piece of your company. How can you do this?" He said, "Well, that part of the company is not going to go anywhere. Our future lies in those two-thirds, and we have to see ourselves capable of rationalizing between what we should put in the United States and what we should put in Canada. A free trade agreement would give us that direction to allow us to make those investment decisions."

An agreement was also needed to reduce trade disputes, and this became the key sticking point in the negotiation with the United States. We had seen a period leading up to this when we would be subject to trade disputes with the United States, molded largely by congressional pressure. What we felt was that, if we were going to go into an agreement with a country ten times our size, we had to have a dispute settlement mechanism where disputes would be settled by impartial bodies that would be based on the facts, rather than simply driven by politics.

The dialogue that we had within Canada during this period leading up to the final agreement was a very broad dialogue. We had ITAC (International Trade Advisory Committee) and SAGIT (Sectoral

Advisory Group on International Trade). These were the principle consultative bodies and were very important in the advice that the negotiators would receive. The political debate itself was on economic issues, social policy implications, and the national interest, the national sovereignty, things like that.

These were the sorts of debates that we had, and they centered on those issues that Mulroney identified in his earlier announcement. But to that, we added water. People were terrified that we would have water directed out of the Great Lakes into other parts of the United States, or that we would be forced to redirect waters in western Canada so that they would be largely serving the interests of the United States. Agriculture became very important and there were also fears that we would have a managed foreign exchange agreement with the United States, which naturally would accrue to the favor of the United States rather than Canada.

Key issues were dairy and poultry, wine, textiles and clothing, softwood lumber (which did not become part of the agreement, but continued to be a narrative between the two countries). Rules of origin were an important part of that as well.

We had a deadline, which was October 3, 1987, and that was because of the Fast Track authority, where we had an up-or-down vote in the United States. We entered into negotiations. The negotiators were having a hard time in the early stages, and it became more and more clear that there was no love lost between Simon Reisman and Peter Murphy.[2] Things just came to a halt. I remember having some intense discussions with (then treasury secretary) Jim Baker and I said, "Jim, you have to get into this. It is not going anywhere." And he said, "Relax, Mike, we work to deadlines in this town. We will be sitting across the table from each other on October 2, and we will get this done by deadline October 3." Sure enough, we were sitting across the table. He was brought in by President Reagan, and Derek Burney[3] and I were brought in by Prime Minister Mulroney to try and conclude the agreement.

---

2. Simon Reisman was chief negotiator for Canada; Peter Murphy was his US counterpart.
3. Canadian ambassador to the United States.

Periodically, during those last two days, Baker would leave the room. And partway through, he told me that he went to speak to Dan Rostenkowski and Sam Gibbons, the two senior Democrats on trade agreements from their position on the House Ways and Means Committee. That was very important in giving him the confidence to be able to accept this or reject that. I was on a platform with Jim about a year ago and I reminded Jim that he was doing this and he smiled. I said, "In today's environment in the United States Congress, would you be able to do that?" And he said, "No, I couldn't." Now that is hugely significant for us as a neighbor to the United States. Some people think that all the things that are happening in the United States only matter to the United States. If we had not had that free trade agreement, our country would be a very different place than it is today. So that ability of the two parties to have a dialogue during the course of that conversation was extraordinarily important to us as a country.

George P. Shultz: I think Jim gave you a wrong answer. If he were there today, working for President Reagan in a Reagan administration, he could have done that. We have an entirely different executive now.

Wilson: Fast forward now to 6:30 on the night of October 3. We had five-and-a-half hours to the deadline, and we reached a deadlock on the dispute settlement agreement. We broke. A few of us got on the phone with the prime minister, we told him where it all was, and we said we do not think he can accept this. He agreed. He said, "You'd better go and speak to Baker and tell him that we will put it to bed. But let's try and do it in the right way. I'd like to speak to the president to put it to bed as nicely as possible."

I went to see Baker. He agreed, and he said, "Well, let's give it another try." In addition—I didn't realize it at the time—Mulroney was not able to get through to the president. But he picked up the phone and called Baker and said, "How are you going to explain to your people that you can get a nuclear arms agreement with your worst enemy, the USSR, and you can't get a goddamned free trade agreement with your best friends, the Canadians?" That, I think, was a significant factor in getting us over the top, because we did get the dispute settlement mechanism, and everything moved nicely from there.

This led right into the general election about a year later, and it was a fierce election. I had intended to step down after ten years in the Parliament. With this election coming up, with the emotions, the passion, and being right in the middle of the final stages, I thought I could not leave. But this will give you the flavor of the election. We had also talked about a goods and services tax, the value-added tax, and that never got into the election campaign. To me, it should have gotten in, because it was pretty controversial, but I just make that point that the focus was entirely on the free trade agreement. And to this day, it's called the free trade election.

Conservatives were obviously in favor, and both the opposition parties were opposed. There were the first stages of negative advertising in our country in that election, and it was a very passionate campaign. We would have the opposition politicians going into nursing homes and saying, "You are going to lose your health care. You are not going to have this nursing home." It got to be very bitter.

There are some quotes that will give you a sense that the future of the country was at stake, according to the national newspapers in Canada. "We said we are going to build a nation." The Liberals said, "You sold us out. You destroyed a 120-year-old dream called Canada. You are surrendering one by one our levers of economic independence." "Made in Ottawa, not in Washington." "It is bad for everyone. It has to be rejected."

I had one very strong supporter, and she had a house right opposite one of our major schools, which is where we were going to have a big candidates' meeting. I went to her and I said, "In the last three elections, you let me put a great big four-by-eight sign on your front lawn." She looked at me and she said, "I can't do it, Mike. You have given our country away." That was the sense that we had during that time.

We won the election. We were in third place with two weeks to go, and Mulroney was told to be a statesman. Just talk about the importance of it to the country and be a statesman. Well, we were in third place, two weeks to go, and he said, "To hell with being a statesman, we've got to fight for this thing." He just took his jacket off, very passionate, saying how important this was, that it was essential for the country to have, and we won a very strong majority. We got 171 seats in a 284-seat House. So it was a very prominent victory.

After that, things settled down, and by the time the discussion of NAFTA came, there was a pretty good acceptance of free trade. The Liberals had opposed the free trade agreement with the United States when they won the election of November 1993; but within days, they reversed their position on trade.

There are people who disagree and come up with some analysis that suggests that the free trade agreement did not do a whole lot for Canada. To the people that say that, I would say that a lot of things have happened since 1988. Whether it's globalization, the recessions that we have had, the Asian crisis, the dot-com bubble, the financial and economic crisis of 2008–2009, or other things that have happened, it is very hard to separate that out and identify the effect of the free trade agreement. The point that I make is, where would Canada be today if we didn't have that free trade agreement? It led to a major transformation of our economy; it is much more competitive, a much more modern economy today than it would have been. Our productivity moved up every year in the '90s. It has leveled off since, but we moved ourselves into a new level of competitiveness. We were able to balance our budget. Our overall current account deficit in trade moved to a surplus. We had current account deficits in the '80s of 4 percent of GDP. In the latter part of the '90s, it moved to a surplus. Exports during the '80s to the United States were about $100 billion a year. By the year 2000, they were $350 billion a year.

Exports as a percentage of GDP moved from about 25 percent to 40 percent, and some years even a good deal higher than that. So, if we did not have the free trade agreement, Canada would have been left with a very weak, fragmented economy, and one that I think would have a significantly lower standard of living. In addition to that, we have a much more confident business community that is looking to expand trade far outside the NAFTA parameters, and I do not think that would have happened if they had not developed the self-confidence they have of being able to be in the most competitive economy in the world.

Carla A. Hills: Let me talk about some of the challenges and opportunities that the North American Free Trade Agreement produced. I have to give credit to Jaime Serra, who raised the subject, not of the NAFTA, but of a bilateral agreement between the United States and Mexico, in Davos in January 1990. As we met in Davos,[4] the US economy was not in robust circumstances. It is a fact that when the economy is down, that stokes economic nationalism. We had been through a battle with Canada over our free trade agreement with it, which almost brought the Mulroney government down.

I brought home from Davos the idea of a free trade agreement with Mexico to the president. I thought it was a good idea. I supported the notion that we expand free trade to all of North America. The president was receptive. We had extensive internal discussions with some yeas and some nays in the administration. But during the months of February and March 1990, we got primary support within the White House and among my cabinet colleagues.

However, some pointed out, are we really taking on more than we can do? We are negotiating the Uruguay Round (of the General Agreement on Tariffs and Trade), which is our top priority, and now we are talking about adding a major bilateral agreement. But in enumerating the many challenges, I would say the number one challenge was to secure Fast Track legislation prior to beginning negotiations. (Mexican) President Salinas made it very clear to President Bush that he wanted the same Fast Track procedures governing the bilateral agreement as Canada and Israel had had with the United States.

Fast Track was a law passed in 1974, signed by President Ford, that was an accommodation to deal with the separation of powers in our government. Our Congress has the power over the purse strings, tariffs, taxes, and the like. The president has the power to negotiate with foreign governments. Under the law, as it was passed, if the president decides to negotiate a trade agreement—bilateral, plurilateral,

---

4. The meeting was the World Economic Forum.

or multilateral—he must notify the Congress. After notification, the Congress has sixty legislative days in which to deny the Fast Track procedures, which require Congress to vote for or against the negotiated agreement when presented without amending it. Sixty legislative days work out to be about four or five months. So if Congress does not vote Fast Track down, the administration has that authority after the sixty legislative days have passed.

Once we decided that we wanted to have a negotiation with Mexico, we had to go to work not only on the content of the negotiation but also on persuading members of Congress that this was a worthy negotiation deserving of Fast Track procedures. And we met a lot of headwind, no question about it. We worked with the two chairs of the relevant committees—Senator Lloyd Bentsen, chair of the Senate Finance Committee, and Congressman Dan Rostenkowski, chair of the Ways and Means Committee—and all members of those committees, since they had primary jurisdiction over trade.

We were facing election in 1992, so we knew that two years out, some of these members were going to be facing even more headwinds at home if we reached an agreement. So we activated our presidential advisory groups in the United States. We had about nineteen presidential advisory groups on trade, and we got businesses activated to explain the merits of an agreement with Mexico. I personally met with all 535 members of Congress and tried to talk to each of them and, more importantly, to listen to what their concerns were. And even when their concerns were wildly off base economically, I would say, "You know, Congressman, that's truly an interesting idea that never occurred to me, and I won't forget it."

By the time we got to August 1990, the two presidents were able to sign a joint agreement that they were thinking positively about a bilateral agreement. They could not officially say they were going to move forward because that would have triggered the Fast Track process. The next day, Jaime and I issued a report that said a bilateral agreement was a good idea, and our recommendation to our presidents was to move forward.

Now this was in August, and our Congress was in recess. So President Bush in September officially notified Congress that he wanted to move forward on the bilateral agreement, and that triggered the sixty legislative days during which they could deny him Fast Track authority.

It was just about that time that we got a call from Canada. Michael Wilson's predecessor, John Crosbie, a wonderful man from Newfoundland, called me and said, "Carla, what about Canada? We want to join." I said, "John, you just went through an election that almost brought the government down. You don't want to join." He said, "Yes, I do. I do not wish to be left out." Then, of course, Mulroney called Bush, and there was a discussion on how do we deal with this. We did not want to offend our very best friend on our northern border, but we did want to move forward. And so we decided, Jaime Serra and I, to invite John Crosbie to dinner in New York, where we had a robust discussion about whether Canada could stand the heat, and the subjects that we would cover in a trilateral trade agreement.

At the end of the dinner, we decided to issue a press release that said the three governments were going to move forward to negotiate a trilateral agreement, but if one of the governments decided to pull out anywhere along the line, the other two would move forward. We did not mention Canada, but we wanted to make clear that the negotiation was going to go forward—bilaterally or trilaterally.

On February 5, 1991, President Bush, President Salinas, and Prime Minister Mulroney issued a press announcement of an intent to negotiate the NAFTA, and immediately, the Senate Finance Committee and Ways and Means Committee held public hearings. About twenty days later, the sixty legislative days governing Fast Track authority had expired without congressional denial, which was good news. But that authority covered our bilateral agreement, not our trilateral agreement. So, challenge number two was to expand Fast Track and to get an extension of two years to enable us to complete the negotiation.

President Bush moved forward and asked for the Fast Track to run until June 1, 1993, which got us over the November 1992 election. The request included Canada, but it did give Congress another opportunity to block the negotiations.

It was about a week later that House Majority Leader Richard Gephardt sent us a ten-page, single-spaced letter outlining his numerous objections and concerns about the agreement. The letter covered labor, environment, autos, agriculture, jobs. You name it—it was on the list. Both Chairmen Rostenkowski and Bentsen had sent earlier letters that were more manageable, but we had to get the Gephardt letter answered and talk about how we were going to deal with the politics going forward. We intensified our meetings with Congress. I think it was extremely important to the success of this trilateral negotiation that we spent so much time with Congress. It was necessary to keep them apprised, particularly those who were going to be forceful supporters. We had numerous executive sessions, which were not publicized, with the Ways and Means and the Finance committees.

Finally, June 1, 1991, arrived. The sixty legislative days had passed, giving us Fast Track authority to negotiate an agreement with both Mexico and Canada. The official negotiation started on June 12, 1991. The next challenge occurred as we tried to negotiate the agreement and to keep the parties who were concerned about the negotiation apprised. We spoke at the Governor's Conference in Seattle. We took eleven members of Congress and twenty-six members of the Private Sector Advisory Group on Trade down to Mexico City to meet with President Salinas. We had hundreds of meetings with various interest groups. I personally spoke to the textile manufacturing association. I got booed, but I said, "You know, we will have a long transition, and this is something that you will benefit from in the long run." To negotiate acceptance, not great support, was to talk about the transition. This was not going to hit tomorrow where the businesses couldn't adapt, but we would deal with these issues, and similarly so, of course, would Mexico.

The tough issues were on autos. We were pushing very hard for 65 percent of NAFTA content, duty drawbacks, the opening of services, particularly including banking and insurance, the limiting of screening of investments, which Canada also did. That is, if you wanted to have a merger or an acquisition, it could be screened, which we felt was very contrary to the free market system. But by August 1992, fourteen months to the day that we began the negotiations, we shook hands in agreement. It was the first comprehensive free trade agreement that had been negotiated between developed and developing countries. It achieved broader and deeper market openings than any prior trade agreement. It opened markets by eliminating tariffs on all industrial goods, guaranteeing unrestricted access of agricultural trade between the United States and Mexico. (Canada did not participate in the agricultural market opening).

It opened a broad range of services, including financial services, and created national treatment for cross-border service providers. It provided high standards to protect patents, trademarks, copyrights, trade secrets, and it was the first trade agreement to do that anywhere in the world. It also prohibited barriers such as local content and import substitution, which were heavily prevalent in the economies that we were negotiating with.

The final challenge was to move the agreement to signature by the heads of the three governments. The Fast Track legislation set forth rules governing when the president could sign the agreement. After we shook hands in August 1992, President Bush lost the election in November. A number of steps were required before he could sign the agreement and leave it to his successor to obtain congressional approval. He could not get it approved by Congress, because of the Fast Track timing rules. Under the legislation, the US Private Sector Advisory Groups, each of them, I think there were nineteen, had to prepare a report for the Congress and for the public on the merits of each of the sections of the agreement. In addition, an overall report on the merits of the agreement was required from the president's Private Sector Advisory Group on trade. It took some time for them to prepare those reports. It was not until the reports were available to Congress—and that meant all of them—that the president could give Congress his notice of intent to sign, and he could not sign until ninety days after giving the notice, which he did give. In December 1992, the president was able, with the expiration of that ninety-day period, to sign the NAFTA. At that point we left it to our successors to get the agreement approved, and they did a magnificent job, in our opinion.

And just to mention the opportunities: one of the great opportunities, of course, was working with great people like Michael Wilson and John Crosbie in Canada and Jaime Serra in Mexico, and we have all become fast friends. Twenty years later, we are even better friends than we were around the conference table.

But aside from that, one big plus was that the NAFTA was a catalyst to multilateralism. Economists worry today that the proliferation of bilateral and plurilateral[5] agreements is destroying multilateralism. After the Uruguay Round collapsed in Brussels in 1990, we began this negotiation of the NAFTA in June 1991, completing it in August 1992. Within four months after Congress had approved the agreement and in 1994, all 123 trade ministers were back at the table at the Uruguay Round, completed that negotiation, and created the World Trade Organization. I believe in "competitive liberalization." There is no question that a high quality major agreement today, as the NAFTA was in 1994, could cause multilateralism to take a giant leap forward once again. So, the NAFTA was a benefit in its own right, but it was also a catalyst for multilateralism.

Jaime Serra Puche: I am going to try to avoid repetition, but I will try to clarify certain things. First, the economic rationale for Mexico: it was not just that Salinas and I woke up one morning in Davos and said, "Oh, let's have a free trade agreement."

Mexico had been a highly protectionist economy for five or six decades. Mexico joined GATT in 1986, forty years after it was created. So it took us forty years to understand that we had to belong to GATT. We had introduced huge distortions in our trade, in relative prices, and we were not competitive. So, when we came into power, we said we have to further liberalize, and we put together a project that was partly a stabilization program, partly a competitiveness-oriented or export-oriented program. We announced it at the beginning of the six-year term. We thought that it would be really welcomed by the rest of the world, but when we went to Davos a few months later, we were facing lukewarm reactions. They said, "These guys have a long way to go."

The wall in Berlin had just fallen, so people were looking at the Eastern European countries. At the end of one evening, very late at

---

5. A plurilateral treaty is a special subset of multilateral treaties in which reservations by one party must be consented to by all the parties.

night, Salinas came to my room and said, "We have to do something. We are not on the map for foreign direct investment. Why don't we start thinking about this idea of trade with the US?" I said, "I have this meeting with Carla tomorrow morning to discuss the textile quotas (our trade was then conducted separately in many sectors, each with specific quotas). I can at least ask my deputy to talk to her deputy and I can talk to her about this." So that's what we did. So that's when I presented the idea to Carla of a Mexico-US free trade agreement. Let me go back to the economic rationale. There were three economic rationales for that decision.

First, as I have said, Mexico was not on the world map for direct investment and we needed foreign investment badly, because we did not generate enough domestic savings to support growth.

Second, we were the number one user of the Generalized System of Preferences (GSP) with the US, which means, for example, that we could export up to 100,000 microphones to the US, paying no tariff. But that system says that if we export 100,000 plus one, you lose the preference for the whole 100,000 microphones every year. So we had a perverse situation in Mexico. Plants that were exporting would close in October because they did not want to lose the preference and they did not want to accumulate inventories. Many plants that were export-ing refrigerators or TVs were closing in October instead of keeping up production in order to avoid these costs.

And the third issue we had was that we had to negotiate, annu-ally or biannually, the quotas for the central agreement. So, exporters could say, "Well, how good are these negotiations going to be this year? As I don't know how the negotiations will go this year, I'd better not invest more." Even when we had reached a good level of exports, we were stuck because of these distortions. Having an agreement with NAFTA was an opportunity to consolidate all the discounts of the GSP and to eliminate all the sectoral agreements. And that actually resulted in a huge incentive for our exporting system.

So the economic rationale was: let's do NAFTA because we need to be on the world map for foreign investment and to get rid of the distortions of the GSP and sectoral agreements. And this will give an impulse to our exporters and manufacturers to grow dramatically into the US market.

After the Davos meeting, several things happened. There was no way we would have gone into that negotiation without Fast Track. I am extremely surprised that the Trans-Pacific Partnership (TPP) countries are negotiating[6] without Fast Track authority. The Fast Track authority is more important for the other negotiating countries than for the US, and that has to be understood properly. Thus, Fast Track was very important for Mexico, probably more important than it was for the US government. We participated for the first time in the lobbying effort. Fast Track (now Trade Promotion Authority) has nothing to do with timing; it has to do with an up-or-down vote, without amendment.

I was preparing for our first ministerial meeting, and I received a phone call from the Canadian ambassador in Mexico, David Winfield. Three or four months before this, Salinas, Mulroney, and I had a conversation, and I told Prime Minister Mulroney that it would be wonderful to have a trilateral agreement. The rationale for Mexico was to not be alone against the elephant. But Mulroney told us, "No way, we just had our election. It was very close, and the FTA was in the center of the debate. But we will give you all sorts of advice."

Then, with three weeks to go to our first meeting, the Canadian ambassador called me and said they want to be on the table. And I said, "But three months ago, your prime minister told us he didn't want to get involved in that any more." He said, "Things have changed, we want to be there."

Apparently, what happened in Canada is that an article was published saying that if Canada was not part of NAFTA, then the US will be the hub of the whole region and would have an advantage over the other two countries. So we agreed to include the Canadians and made an announcement about the three-party negotiations, saying that if one party stepped down, the agreement with the other two countries would stay in force. The three ministers signed a letter to this effect.

---

6. Referring to twelve-nation Trans-Pacific Partnership conference in Singapore, December 7–10, 2013.

Our concern was that the Canadians might want to be party-poopers and would not want the Mexicans to have the same preferences as the Canadians for access to the US market, but this was not the case. The negotiation was exemplary in terms of the relationship among the three countries. (Sometimes Michael and I ganged up on Miss Carla, sometimes Carla and Michael ganged up against us, but it was an equitable process.)

There is another issue which is very relevant: the politics changed dramatically in the US when Bush lost the election, Clinton won the election. During the campaign the position of the Clinton team was not very in favor of a NAFTA agreement. Politically they had a very complicated situation. The negotiation under Bush was a complicated negotiation but, in a way, it was simple because we had an agreement on where we wanted to get to. We knew that we wanted a free trade agreement with no tariffs, with no obstacles to trade, with investment chapters, with intellectual property, with dispute settlement. So a good chunk of the negotiation was how to get there, the transition period. Among other things, the Canadians stayed out of agriculture, we stayed out of energy, and the Americans kept maritime transportation. Except for a few things like that, there was a clear understanding of what we wanted to achieve.

For the second part of the negotiation, under Clinton, the politics around the trade agreement were different. That is where the contributions by Mickey Kantor, Bill Daley, and Ron Brown[7] came in. Our perception was that the side agreements on the environment and labor were a new element of protectionism facing Mexican products. It took us almost a year to negotiate the two side agreements, compared to thirteen or fourteen months to negotiate the main text. If I remember properly, we proposed that the side agreement would incorporate labor and the environment, but the premise of that negotiation would be: "Let's not change the text that is already signed and agreed upon." Fortunately, the Clinton administration, under Mickey's leadership, agreed with that. That was a huge step that facilitated the

---

7. At the time, Kantor was US Trade Representative; Brown was secretary of commerce; and Daley was special counsel to the president for NAFTA.

negotiation, because if we had reopened the text that we had approved a few months before, it would have been a very complicated negotiation, possibly the end of the whole process. I remember at one point when Mickey told me that the agreement was not going to fly with his friend Dick Gephardt. I told Mickey, "Listen. This is such a big issue in Mexico that if it fails, we have to agree on how to announce it, because we are going to have anti-US demonstrations in Mexico. And probably we will actually push for some demonstrations to do some face-saving." We weren't as elegant as you guys when Mulroney talked to Baker. But we did not have to go through that radical scenario. I think it worked out nicely.

Shultz: I'd like to ask a question because several times people said that the US-Canada agreement almost brought down the Mulroney government. But, if I'm not mistaken, what you told us, Michael, was that it was just going along in the election period and then when Brian took off the gloves and went campaigning heavily on it, he wound up winning by a landslide.

Wilson: The early part of the campaign, as I said earlier, was all free trade and it was very negative. So we were having a great deal of difficulty. And as you said, Mulroney was trying to stand above the fight and be a statesman. In the end, he said, "If I do that, we're just going to get swamped. I've got to demonstrate to people—the Canadians—that this is really important to us and I'm going to fight till the end on it." If he hadn't, we wouldn't have won that election.

Shultz: Yes, but he did. And he won by a landslide. So, somehow this is very defensible material if you will get out and fight.

Daniel Trefler: I think it is more complicated because essentially the popular vote was only about 40 percent.

Wilson: Dan is absolutely right. The Liberals and the NDP split the vote. It's rare that with three parties any party will get more than 45 percent of the vote.

Mickey Kantor: We had about one-third support in the country for NAFTA in the summer of '93, by polls. Bill Clinton decided that he would go and fight for it publicly. And, not just because of his ability, but also (Vice President) Al Gore and others going out to the public changed that to two-thirds support by the time we finished our negotiation in November and got the NAFTA through Congress. So you're absolutely correct about that. We sometimes shy away from these arguments because we think the public won't go with us and in fact the public did.

Hills: President Clinton reached out. I can recall him personally calling me and asking me to come to the East Room where he had it filled with members of Congress from both parties. And he had invited about five participants to say why every American should be in favor of the NAFTA.

Kantor: Well, that was a session when he had President George H. W. Bush, Bush '41, who is by the way a terrific guy and was a great president. I and President Clinton admire him so much for what he did—not just in trade, but many other areas. All of the living presidents were there in the East Room to support the NAFTA, because Clinton decided the only way to win this was to go at it directly. It ended up with Al Gore debating (former presidential candidate) Ross Perot on the Larry King Show in November. Secretary Shultz makes an important point about taking this to the public and not being afraid of these issues.

Michael Boskin: I would just add—and then, Mickey, go ahead and give us your perspective on getting it through Congress—that it was a very conscious decision on the part of the Bush campaign in 1988 to run as a free trader. And he won overwhelmingly, and he decided to confront that head-on. So, often you can change opinion if you get out and do the explanation. From my perspective as an academic, the intellectual debate over free trade really has to be fought over and over again. The gain from trade which we teach to our economics students is a very subtle concept to most people. A lot of people start with the assumption that one side is getting something and the other side is therefore losing it. So I think you can't underestimate that. Most people aren't thinking about it if it's not their own direct interest. You have to get out and make that campaign. That's been going on in economic and political history since the debates over the Corn Laws[8] and their repeal.

Kantor: In trade in the US, we stand on each other's shoulders— Democrats and Republicans. No one does this alone. If you look at the Uruguay Round or NAFTA, it finished in the Clinton administration, but it started with the Bush administration. If you look at what's going on with TPP now, it started in the Bush administration, and it's being finished in the Obama administration. So the fact is, it is a bipartisan, almost nonpartisan, activity. And it's best that way, because if it becomes politicized it's not very effective.

Let me go back to the '92 campaign because of a misperception. Bill Clinton made a speech at North Carolina State on October 4, 1992. What he said was the following: "I am for NAFTA, but I want labor and environment agreements." That's a short statement. Bill Clinton doesn't make statements that short. We had a huge fight in the campaign over whether or not he should be for NAFTA. Ohio and Michigan were critical and they were anti-NAFTA states. No Republican has ever won the presidency without winning Ohio— ever. And we needed to win Ohio. But Bill Clinton finally ended the debate in the campaign, saying, "I'm going to be for it, but I'm going to say we need labor and environment side agreements because I don't believe I can get it through Congress without them," and I think he was correct about that.

Fast forward; now he makes a big speech at American University in February. We start the negotiation over side agreements in February of '93. During those negotiations Bill Clinton was involved, I would say, in every nit and jot of that situation. He's someone who reads everything. And he was involved in these issues and deeply committed to

---

8. The Corn Laws were a set of protectionist British trade laws for grain, passed by Parliament in 1815 and repealed in 1846.

getting it done. We, of course, were talking to Pat Moynihan, then chairman of the Senate Finance Committee. Lloyd Bentsen was our secretary of the Treasury when Pat took over Finance. And Danny Rostenkowski was still at Ways and Means. He was a tremendous help in this.

Our agreement with the Republicans was as follows—and it hasn't been talked about much. We were told they would not deliver a Republican vote—and I don't blame them—unless we got at least one hundred Democrats in the House to vote for it. The House was the critical body; the Senate was done, but the House wasn't. So we had to deliver one hundred Democrats. So what we did was have, in the Roosevelt Room, day after day after day—beginning in September, after the event you talked about, Carla—members of Congress come in. The president would talk to them about how important this was. One of the interesting questions he asked—especially Democrats— was, "If you could vote secretly, how would you vote?" Well, everyone said, "Of course, we'd be for it." He said, "Doesn't that tell you something?" You know, basically, "Come on. We have got to do this. It's for the good of the country. We're tying these three countries together. We're changing trade agreements as we know them. This will be a template for trade forever. We want to foster free trade, rules-based trade around the world, and we can't do it without getting this done. We can't get beat."

And it really culminated, as I said, with the Gore-Perot debate. We ended up getting 102 Democrats. We had 232 votes in the House— 130 Republicans and 102 Democrats. We breathed a sigh of relief. The Florida delegation, all seventeen members, said, "We're not voting for this unless you change some of these rules at EPA (Environmental Protection Agency) over the use of herbicides and pesticides." It was a headache for us because Democrats are environmentalists. Finally, President Clinton said to me, "Open the candy store." He said, "We have got to get this done. If that's what they need, get it done."

Anyway, I called the head of the EPA (Carol Browner) and I thought she was going to faint over the phone. "Gasp—you're going to do what? You want us to do what?" And so we did. And we got the seventeen votes. Without that we wouldn't have had 102 and, by the way, I think the Republicans would have walked on us.

Shultz: This was an instance of something unrelated to the agreement, which they wanted, which is not an unusual tactic.

Kantor: Absolutely. We ended the Uruguay Round one month after we got the vote in Congress on the NAFTA. The two of them came within thirty days of each other. In the middle we had the meeting putting together the APEC (Asia-Pacific Economic Cooperation) for the first time with all the leaders in Seattle.

You cannot get these agreements if you don't have someone across the table you can work with who understands your politics, and you try to understand their politics. Right at the end, I got a call from the new (Canadian) prime minister, Jean Chrétien, who said, "We can't do this." I said, "You can't do what?" "We can't do the NAFTA." I said, "Wait, wait, wait! We're right on the edge of Congress voting. What do you mean you can't?" He said, "Well, there's some things we just don't like." So, I went up to see (Minister for International Trade) Roy MacLaren. We sat, and we put our heads together and talked to the prime minister, and finally they agreed that they would go along with NAFTA. Their politics were quite different from the preceding government's, but they came through in the end.

There was a lot of political courage in this on all sides. I give great credit to them. I give great credit to Bill Clinton. We did not have a political party that was for free trade, to say the least. And Bill Clinton, from his speeches in 1991 at Georgetown all the way through, never faltered in his support for rules-based trade and the need to move this forward. So I give him enormous credit for what he did. But President Bush and Bill Clinton—who've become fast friends, as you know, in subsequent years and work together on a number of issues around the world—always agreed on this issue. We won Ohio and Michigan by plenty—thank goodness, or we couldn't have won the election—in spite of the fact that he had taken a position for NAFTA. But he had to put in the nuances of labor and environment in order to satisfy certain concerns.

There were three hundred trade agreements made in eight years in the Clinton administration. The momentum was there, and I regret the fact that we lost momentum after that to some degree. Hopefully, it's coming back now with TPP and TTIP with the Europeans. But if we don't get Fast Track (Trade Promotion Authority), you can forget it.

Serra Puche: Why don't you tell us a little bit about the dinner in the White House—the dinner before the long weekend before the vote? You guys organized a dinner and you invited many congressmen to the White House. These guys were going back to their districts, and were being picked on, and were changing from yes to no. President Clinton organized a dinner with congressmen to make sure those guys had an excuse not to go back to the district. I thought it was a good move.

Kantor: Absolutely, keep them away from the district because they were being pressured.

Boskin: That stands in contrast to the current president's management style. NAFTA became kind of the bogeyman of trade. It became the lead item on the complaint list for the anti-globalization, anti-trade, anti-capitalism folks, and a lot of demonstrations resulted. It eventually assumed almost mythic proportions. Ross Perot had his "giant sucking sound." Mickey mentioned that there was even a larger protectionist or anti-trade cohort in the Democratic Party. But Republicans have one, too, as (former presidential candidate) Pat Buchanan demonstrated. But it's even larger in the Democratic Party. In 2008, candidate Obama said he would tear up NAFTA, which was a remarkable statement. Fortunately, he's come around to support of trade liberalization. One of the reasons it's important to get it right is that all the myth, all the urban legend, about NAFTA that's out there tends to be what ordinary people digest. They watch the evening news and they see a demonstration. Well, there must be something going on, right?

So it is really important to mobilize support, to enable congressmen—many of whom don't know much economics or haven't studied it in a long time—to understand and explain the case for free trade.

Chapter Two

Mexico and Canada Before and After NAFTA

NAFTA altered the course of the Mexican and Canadian economies by opening them up to greater competition for a share of the United States' large and demanding market. Political scientist Stephen Haber and economist Daniel Trefler examine why open borders and energy markets are politically difficult issues and why they should still be up for discussion in the future.

Presenters: Stephen Haber, Daniel Trefler
Comments: John B. Taylor, George P. Shultz, Michael H. Wilson, Carla A. Hills, Jaime Serra Puche, Michael J. Boskin, Lorenzo Caliendo

John Taylor: It is fascinating listening to Carla, Mickey, and Jaime, the people who actually negotiated NAFTA, and to get their perspectives on the politics and details. I remember coming back with Carla from Brussels (in 1990) and that disappointing Uruguay Round negotiation when she wisely insisted that, "This is not going to work." Because of that insistence, just a few years later, a much better agreement was signed. That's a very important prelude to this whole NAFTA story.

I also note that this year is not only the twentieth anniversary of NAFTA, it is also the twentieth anniversary of central bank independence in Mexico. I don't think these two moves toward rules-based policy are a coincidence. They are both pretty much the same drive to improved economic policy.

It is true that market opening is slowing down now, perhaps because of 9/11.[1] I was in the government on 9/11 and saw another more

---

1. September 11, 2001, terrorist attacks on New York City and Washington, DC.

optimistic part of this story. I think without the structure of NAFTA, the negative impact on trade could have been a lot worse.

Stephen Haber: I have been traveling to Mexico now for over forty years and to see the change that has occurred in Mexico in the last twenty is truly remarkable. The effects of NAFTA go well beyond free trade. In fact, NAFTA had several unanticipated consequences, some of which have already been hinted at, for example, by John when he says it's also the twentieth anniversary of central bank independence.

NAFTA opened up a process in Mexico that resulted in Mexico's democratization. It wasn't the intention of Carlos Salinas to do that. He was trying in fact to get his political party, the PRI,[2] to hold on. But it set in motion a process that in fact became politically very difficult to control and that redounded to the benefit of Mexican society.

Prior to the 1990s, Mexico wasn't just closed to foreign trade; Mexico was closed to competition, period. The Mexican economy from the 1890s all the way to the 1990s was one huge cartel. In the post-revolutionary period, after the 1920s, you basically have a coalition of organized labor, public employees, factory owners, and politicians. It wins elections for a single party—the PRI—and then protects the country against foreign trade with extremely high tariff barriers and nontariff barriers and protects the manufacturers from competition through a whole range of cartel-like arrangements. My favorite was the import permit program, where if you wanted to import machinery into Mexico you had to get a permit. But, you couldn't apply for the permit until you imported the machinery, which meant that if you didn't know somebody in the government you imported the machinery and then it sat in customs for whoever knows how long.

You needed permission from the secretary of the Treasury and the president to get a bank charter. What was the structure of the banking system? There were many commercial banks, but in fact four commercial banks controlled about 80 percent of assets. Those same commercial banks owned the non-bank banks called the *financieras,* which mostly lent to the industrial conglomerates that owned

---

2. Partido Revolucionario Institucional (Institutional Revolutionary Party).

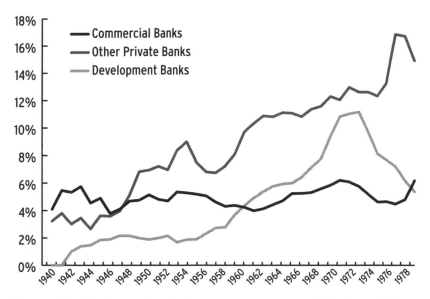

Figure 2.1 Bank lending, by type, as a percent of Mexican GDP, 1940–1978.

Source: Data from INEGI (Instituto Nacional de Estadística y Geografía) Estadísticas históricas de México 2009, table 18.26.

the banks. So the biggest of these, The Legorreta Group—one of the biggest manufacturers in Mexico—also owned the largest bank and the largest *financiera*. That basically meant that access to capital was a barrier to entry.

There was a huge state-owned banking system, government-run banks. Commercial banks lent only about 5 percent of GDP (figure 2.1). Who did the government-owned banks lend to? They lent to the same conglomerates. In fact, in the 1960s the government's industrial finance bank only lent to forty-seven companies. Four of those companies comprised 30 percent of all the lending. So this was a very cartelized economy in which it wasn't just foreign trade that was cut off; all competition was constrained. There were national, industry-wide labor agreements in which manufacturers all paid the same wages across the country. Everything was set up to discourage competition.

This is an equilibrium. It's a way to win elections and create peace in a country that had a very violent revolution in the 1910s. It was very good at that—that is, at creating peace—but very bad at creating economic growth and opportunity. It's not a surprise that, circa 1970, Mexico had amongst the most unequal distributions of income in the world. In fact, only two countries were more unequal: Brazil and South Africa. The South Africans invented apartheid. Mexico was a country that had fought a social revolution to make everybody better off, and yet was highly unequal because of the cartelized nature of the economy.

Following NAFTA, there is a very different equilibrium in Mexico. There is an open, export-driven economy. There are high levels of foreign direct investment, relative to what they were before, and sustained growth, although not at breakneck levels. Mexico is financially more open, with increased levels of public goods provision and falling levels of poverty. One of the big winners from NAFTA is the Mexican worker. There is less corruption than there was under the old cartelized arrangement and, most importantly, there is a multiparty democracy. These features are not independent of each other, just as the features of the cartelized Mexican system were not independent of each other. They're components of a general political and economic equilibrium.

NAFTA was not a randomized field experiment. It's part of a process that begins even earlier in the 1980s, as Jaime pointed out, with Mexico's decision to join the GATT. But it's an important part of the shift in Mexico from one equilibrium to another. And it helped push that shift in equilibrium in ways that were not anticipated by President Salinas when he decided to go for free trade.

Economists are in the business of giving advice to politicians about how to make economies grow. Politicians are not in the business of taking their advice. They're in the business of winning elections. The reason why Carlos Salinas took good advice can be seen in figure 2.2, which shows real GDP per capita in 2005 purchasing power from 1974–2012. Compare the pre-NAFTA period with post-NAFTA.

You don't have to run a regression to see that there are two events here. The first is from 1981 to 1988: real per capita GDP in Mexico falls by close to 20 percent, a real wakeup call to the PRI. Since NAFTA, the Mexican economy has started to grow again, with some blips. Carlos Salinas took the advice from his economics team because the

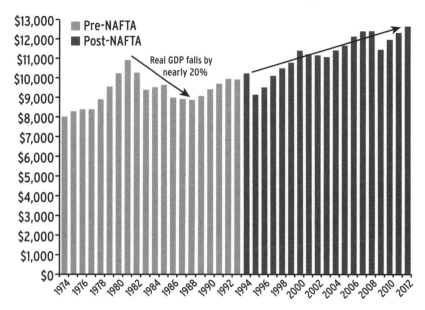

Figure 2.2 Mexican real GDP per capita, 2005 PP$, 1974-2012.
Source: Data from GDP from Alan Heston, Robert Summers, and Bettina Aten, Penn World Table Version 7.1, Center for International Comparisons of Production, Income, and Prices at the University of Pennsylvania, July 2012, https://pwt.sas.upenn.edu/php_site/pwt71/pwt71 _form.php. and World Bank "World Development Indicators," 2013.

economy and real wages were collapsing. Figure 2.3 displays an index of real manufacturing wages in Mexico, data from the International Labor Organization. Real wages fell by about 50 percent from 1981–88. How can you get such a fast fall in real wages?

Part of the core coalition of the PRI was organized labor, which was seeing a dramatic drop in wages. Beginning in the '70s, Mexico started running an inflation tax. And by the 1980s inflation was over 100 percent a year. So the labor leaders had agreed to hold down wage demands. There was an agreement among manufacturers, the government, and the big labor unions to hold down wage demands at the same time that inflation went through the roof. Carlos Salinas faced a big problem in the 1988 election: it was not clear that the PRI, which had run Mexico since the 1930s, was going to survive.

Until the 1960s, the opposition parties were tiny and fragmented. Figure 2.4 shows the proportion of the valid vote won in Mexican

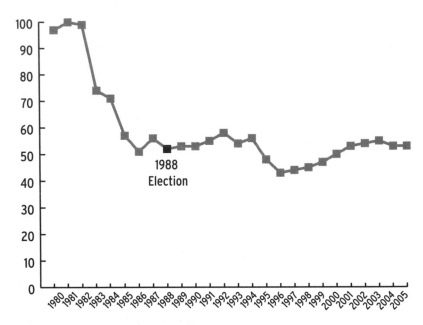

Figure 2.3 Index of real Mexican manufacturing wages, 1981=100.

Source: Stephen Haber, Herbert S. Klein, Noel Maurer, and Kevin J. Middlebrook, *Mexico Since 1980* (New York: Cambridge University Press, 2008).

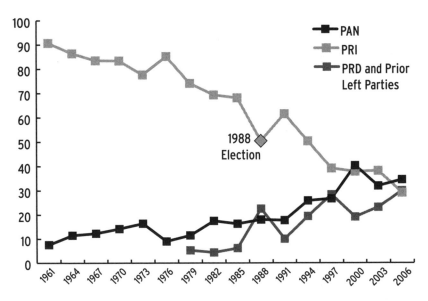

Figure 2.4 Proportion of the valid vote won by each major party, 1960–2006.

Source: Stephen Haber, Herbert S. Klein, Noel Maurer, and Kevin J. Middlebrook, *Mexico Since 1980* (New York: Cambridge University Press, 2008).

presidential elections from 1960 to 2006. The PRI declines; various other parties, which have changed over time, rise. Salinas won in 1988 with just over 50 percent of the vote, an election that was widely accused of being the product of fraud. He probably did really win the election—by the skin of his teeth. On election night, the PRI panicked. When the returns from Mexico City were coming in and the industrial workers who used to vote for the PRI were clearly abandoning the party because their wages were falling, they shut down the computers that were counting the votes. They announced the computers were broken. A day or two later, the PRI announced, "We won." The evidence seems to be that once they turned the computers on again—a couple of weeks later—they actually counted, and Salinas won by a tiny margin. But for the party, this was a disaster. They were in serious trouble.

So Salinas took the advice of his economic advisor, Jaime Serra Puche, and opened up to trade, and investment, and privatization as a fix for the economy and therefore for the PRI. Figure 2.5 shows the huge drop in Mexico's average tariff rate in 1988. Imports subject to permits in the early 1980s were 100 percent . . . a cartel.

Jaime Serra Puche mentioned that NAFTA was not just about free trade; it's also about promoting foreign direct investment. That is really one of the keys to NAFTA. One of the problems that American and Canadian manufacturers had had in Mexico was that there had been a periodic squeeze on the foreigners. Beginning with the (Gustavo) Díaz Ordaz administration in the 1960s, Mexicanization laws were adapted; for example, American firms operating in Mexico had to export at least as much as they imported. Car manufacturers imported automobile parts into Mexico but exported oranges, because they couldn't export cars.

NAFTA got rid of all those kinds of arrangements and gave foreign firms the ability to protect their property rights. US and Canadian firms had to be treated just like Mexican firms.

In some respects, NAFTA accomplished its designed goals. Figure 2.6 shows exports as a percent of GDP from 1960–2012. There is obviously a NAFTA effect. Mexico is now one of the most export-intensive economies in the world; about a third of GDP is

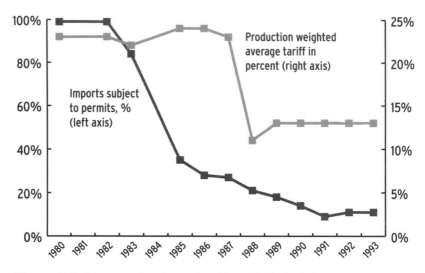

Figure 2.5 Mexican trade protection, 1979–1994.

Source: Stephen Haber, Herbert S. Klein, Noel Maurer, and Kevin J. Middlebrook, *Mexico Since 1980* (New York: Cambridge University Press, 2008).

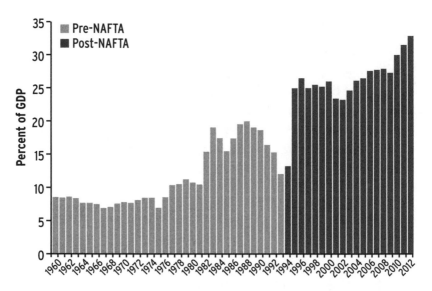

Figure 2.6 Exports as a percent of GDP, Mexico, 1960–2012.

Source: World Bank, "World Development Indicators," 2013.

exports. Mexico had historically been a primary product exporter. Today, Mexico is primarily an exporter of manufactured goods. Automobiles and automobile parts are the number one export. Mexico has even moved into helicopter production. Multinational firms have moved into Mexican manufacturing, particularly in the northern part of the country.

One of the important effects of NAFTA—contrary to the urban legend—is that most of the gains of NAFTA were captured by the Mexican middle class. The pretax, pre-transfer Gini coefficient[3] is falling, a reduction in income inequality in Mexico.

How did Mexico reduce income inequality? It wasn't by taxing the rich out of the country. It was by increasing competition within the country, creating more opportunities. One of the biggest changes NAFTA enabled is the growth of a highly educated Mexican middle class, engineers working for Sikorsky helicopter or Ford Motors. They're working for all the automobile parts manufacturers spread around Mexico.

Foreign direct investment increased post-NAFTA but, relative to the size of the economy, less than was anticipated. On average, the trend rate of growth in the Mexican economy since NAFTA has been 1.1 percent a year in real per capita terms.

Opening up the economy to trade and investment caused a huge disruption. Salinas was gambling that he could create a new coalition to support the PRI because the economy would take off. The economy grew, but it didn't take off. He couldn't put together a new coalition. The manufacturers went to the PAN[4] party. Many of the workers in the protected industries went to the PRD.[5] So what happened was parties like the PAN, which had been a pro-business party going back to the 1940s, grew exponentially in this period and forced a set of changes in Mexico's electoral rules. The PAN won the 2000 election. The PRI lost its control of Congress in 1997 and the presidency in 2000.

---

3. The Gini coefficient is a statistical method for representing a nation's income distribution.
4. Partido Acción Nacional, or National Action Party.
5. Partido de la Revolución Democrática, or Party of the Democratic Revolution.

Beginning in 2000, Mexico started to score at the democratic level on indexes of political democracy. Mexico today has a multiparty democracy in which elections are cleanly run and hard fought. The PRI came back to power in 2012, but it's a very different PRI than the PRI of the 1970s. The first thing the new president did was arrest the head of the teachers' union for corruption.

The final point I want to make here is that one of the effects of NAFTA, unanticipated at the time, was that when you open up an economy it sets in motion a process that may be very difficult to control. The big winners were the Mexican public. No country, except for Singapore, a city-state, has managed to successfully open up and create a competitive economy, in which there is equality of opportunity, and not be democratized. The countries that have opened their economies all tend to democratize, and Mexico is a prime example.

Daniel Trefler: Let me take you back to Canada as it was before the Canadian-American free trade agreement. It was a country that, like Mexico, was sheltered behind a very high tariff wall. And industrial organization in that environment was such that the competitive environment was very weak. Business had figured correctly that if they didn't face any competition, then there was really no point in investing in innovative techniques to survive. So they had no incentive to invest in the new technologies that would more cheaply produce better products, which in turn would allow firms to charge high markups and pay big dividends and salaries and wages.

CUSFTA (the Canada-US Free Trade Agreement) and then NAFTA pulled down that tariff wall. And in doing so, it really improved the competitive environment by both pressuring and supporting Canadian businesses. The support, of course, was improved access to a big market. And not just any old big market, but—and this point applies very much in spades to Mexico—the US market. The US market has these very demanding buyers who come to Canadian firms and say, "You're not doing it well enough and we don't like what you're doing, but here's how you can do it better." And the US likewise has the same sophisticated suppliers—whether they be manufacturers of machinery and equipment, or management consulting firms. The sophisticated suppliers and demanding buyers, they are the ones that are supporting Canadian firms. Balanced against this support is intense competitive pressure to upgrade and face the competition or fold and die.

If we don't think about trade agreements sufficiently in these terms, we won't understand what Canada went through and we won't understand how to take the real lessons of the Canada-US Free Trade Agreement and NAFTA into the next generation of agreements.

Many of our agreements focus on the minutiae of special interest politics. The European Union has a tariff against plastic figurines. And that tariff is zero if it's a human figurine, and it's high if it's a non-human figurine. What do you do with Spock?[6]

But who cares about this kind of minutiae? Why are we being driven by special interests? Where is the big vision about what these agreements are trying to accomplish? I would say that, Stephen, in your talk, you're really hitting on the biggest issue, which is: what does it do to the fabric of society—particularly political and constitutional issues? I think we can make similar comments in the Canadian context as well.

That said, my starting point here is purely economic. Even within very narrowly defined industries, there are huge differences in the performance of firms. There are huge productivity differences, by which I mean the ability of firms to cut costs, to introduce process innovations that are going to find new ways of delivering goods with fewer inputs, but I also mean it in terms of profitability—meaning the ability of firms to find new markets, identify new products that are going to allow them to charge the markups that are really important for both profitability and for workers' success. And you don't have to look far. Compare Apple versus Blackberry. Unfortunately, Canada currently is coming out on the short end of that stick. But there will be other products where we will come out as the winners.

The analysis should reflect the huge amount of research that people like Lorenzo and I and others have been doing to try and understand: what do these agreements do to the underlying economy? In figure 2.7, the horizontal axis is the productivity of firms, and what we

---

6. *Star Trek* character Mister Spock.

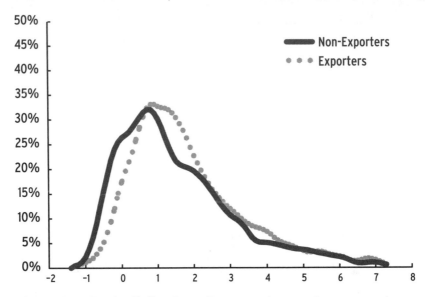

Figure 2.7 Productivity: Canadian exporters and non-exporters.

Source: Marc J. Melitz and Daniel Trefler, "Gains from Trade When Firms Matter," *Journal of Economic Perspectives* 26 (2) (Spring 2012): 91–118.

have represented here is the distribution of productivities in Canadian manufacturing. So we're looking at data for thirty-five thousand Canadian manufacturing firms. The height of these two curves tells you how many firms are in each location in the spectrum of productivity from low productivity to high productivity. Not surprisingly, it looks like a bell curve.

Now compare the exporters and non-exporters. The non-exporters are heavily represented on the left side and tend to be lower-productivity firms. You see the exporters on the right side, the high-productivity spectrum. The US, by giving Canadian firms the opportunity to expand into the US market by lowering its tariffs against Canadian firms, allowed Canada's most productive firms to export and grow. And Canada, by lowering its tariffs against the US, pressured Canadian firms, now facing stiffer competition. And the non-exporters suffered, not able to compete.

So, what's the net effect of that for productivity? When you get to drop your lowest productivity firms and put more weight on your highest productivity firms, there are winners and losers, but overall this is good news for average productivity. That's the first big effect of this agreement. I guess, Michael and Jaime and Carla, that this productivity effect wasn't on your radar screen, because we didn't have the technology to discuss it back then.

The second effect is: what do firms actually do in response? Not only do they grow, but they actually actively work to improve their productivity. And what do they specifically do? Well, we know that there's this wonderful synergy, this complementary reinforcement between exporting and investing in productivity. The point of investing in productivity is to find new products or new ways of producing things cheaper. But that requires upfront investments. How do you find the money for that? If you export, you generate revenues for your firm which support the innovation and increase your market share abroad. So there is a positive feedback. You invest. It makes you more profitable abroad. When you're profitable abroad, you have the funds to do the investments. That synergy can be seen in very fine-grained analysis of firms.

For example, consider the huge improvement in adoption rates of lean manufacturing in Canada—not across the board, but differentially for those firms that saw the tariffs fall on their goods. In other words, those firms that were in the best position to benefit from the agreement because they were facing stiff US tariffs started doing business differently, survived, and improved productivity.

How large is the productivity effect? Consider table 2.1. As we let exporters grow, we raise our average manufacturing productivity by about 4 percent. When less productive firms were forced to exit or to contract, we got another more than 4 percentage points on our manufacturing productivity. The bigger incentive to invest raised productivity by another 5 percent. We reduced tariffs and we increased productivity by 13–14 percent.

Basically, the Canadian economy got about $50 billion of additional output each year. The government gets about $20 billion of that each and every year. To put that in US context, just scale up by ten. It's $200 billion in government coffers every year. That's a lot of fiscal room.

The bottom line is that free trade agreements have very tangible, concrete, rigorously identified, huge positive effects. And to

Table 2.1 Sources of improved productivity

Reallocation	
Growth of exporters (most-productive plants)	4.1%
Contraction and exit of least-productive plants	4.3%
Innovation	
Exporting and innovation synergies	5.4%
Total	
Total	13.8%

Source: Alla Lileeva and Daniel Trefler, "Improved Access to Foreign Markets Raises Plant-Level Productivity . . . for Some Plants," *Quarterly Journal of Economics* 125 (3) (August 2010): 1051–1099.

summarize, the reason we've had those effects is because people like Michael and Carla and Jaime and Mickey went out there, did the right thing, and showed leadership—got ahead of the pack, got ahead of public opinion, and did the right thing.

George P. Shultz: One of the things that impressed me as Carla and others spoke was the immense amount of time you spent consulting with members of Congress. It's an absolute truth that if you want me with you on the landing, include me on the takeoff. If you negotiate something and throw it out to Congress, you're not going to get there. So, I think that's one of the reasons why you succeeded.

Michael H. Wilson: The importance of getting congressional support is more important in the United States than it is in a parliamentary democracy where the governing party controls the outcome. So we never had any concern about getting support from Parliament. The party was basically in support of the leadership. But the ITAC and SAGIT, these were consultative bodies that we had similar to what Carla has described. That really brought onside many parts of the economy because people understood what the agreement was going to be about and what the impacts were going to be on them. It got them onside so that they were supporters and provided a balance from the economic side to all of these rhetorical exaggerations about harm to our social programs, our culture, and national sovereignty. I think that was an extraordinarily important part of it for us to get the final result.

Shultz: But I think it helps you as a negotiator, so it's clear to your opposite number that what you agree to is going to be upheld. We seem to have fallen out of the habit of this kind of consultation. It has to be done across the board and in a bipartisan way.

Carla A. Hills: Congress members have to run for election and need the support of the people to win. So they have to be knowledgeable. And trade agreements are often complicated. So, if they hear from folks in their district that they're going to have a loss of jobs, they have to have the information to counter. When there are prestigious voices speaking against trade, you find the polls on trade sinking. We saw that after the 2008 presidential election, when two respected senators really out-competed each other for "no more trade agreements," "time-out for trade," "no more NAFTAs," "renegotiate the NAFTA." And the polls showed that the American people became frightened of trade, convinced that the opening of foreign markets threatened their jobs.

If we want to double exports, we've got to be active in the global-ized economy. Although today the public seems less anxious to get out on the security side of issues, they seem to be more willing to understand that we have to be a player in the global market. So the antagonism to trade has been reduced somewhat. But I think that we really have to sell the fact that the opening of global markets and the trade agreements that create certainty generate economic growth and jobs. We need the spokespeople who are elected to get out there and explain these issues.

Michael Boskin: We're not a parliamentary democracy, but a republic. And typically the rules of the Senate have allowed very nar-row special interests to block a lot. For example, Carla had to deal with the Carolina senators over textiles. I had to deal with them on such a trivial thing as when President Bush agreed we would double the number of Polish wool women's skirts. The Berlin Wall fell, we had a presidential mission to Poland, and we wanted to do some small things quickly to show our support as they emerged from the shadow of Soviet communism.

There is a famous quote from Senator (Strom) Thurmond: "How can we produce the parachutes for the next invasion if we allow more foreign textiles in?" He was very concerned about losing mills in the Carolinas, as perhaps he should have been, representing those people. So the rules of our system, designed on balance to temper the passions of the age, give very narrow special interests, that are geographically extremely concentrated, a lot of blocking power.

Shultz: (Senator) Russell Long's mantra is better than Strom Thurmond's. Russell said, "I'm against any deal I'm not in on."

Wilson: Quality is an important element of the competitive environment. Our wine growers were absolutely terrified that the growers from the Napa Valley and other places in the United States were just going to kill them. And the politicians, we fell for it and gave them $10 million to pull all their vines out of the ground. But at the same time, the government realized that they had to free up the regulatory process on wines—Canadian-grown wines—to allow them to compete. About three or four years later, I was coming home on a plane from Europe and there was a wine grower, and I asked how things were going—expecting him to punch me in the face. And he said, "Well, look," and he opened up his briefcase, and there were three certificates that he had won in France for the quality of the wines that he was producing in the Niagara region. But what we did was open up the market so that they could bring different grape varieties in and grow better grapes and make better wine.

Shultz: That's Daniel's point in a different way.

Boskin: What didn't work as you anticipated? What do you wish had been included that wasn't? And what do you wish could have been excluded, if that had been possible? Looking back on it, there was an issue of whether it could get political passage, obviously. I was not a big fan of the labor and environment addendum. What would you have liked to have done somewhat differently if the politics would have allowed, or what has surprised you about its implementation?

Hills: I think the NAFTA worked very well. I would have liked to see immigration as part of the agreement. We call that mode four. Had workers been able to come across our border to work and return home, it would have eliminated a lot of the friction over illegal immigrants that we have today. And I would have liked to see energy put on the table. Both were politically impossible: energy for Mexico and immigration for the United States. But as far as what would we have done differently, I don't think of anything that I would have done differently other than maybe expedite the negotiations. If we could have signed the agreement in April of 1992, then we could have enforced it that much earlier, and that would have been something that President Bush would have greatly appreciated.

Jaime Serra Puche: There are three elements of the agreement I would have liked to push further. The first one is the energy chapter, which I think should have been different. As we speak now, the Mexican Congress is discussing a major transformation in the energy sector, which could transform the energy picture in North America. However, my recommendation would not be changing chapter 6 of NAFTA, but creating a collaboration program among the countries that adds to the NAFTA text.

The second one is that we did not have enough instruments to effectively solve disputes. For instance, Mexico has not been able yet to convince the US government to let the trucks cross the border. The logistics are incredibly complicated nowadays. And the agreement was to open the states that neighbor the border first, and keep on opening the rest of the territories. Well, the treatments stopped it and we haven't been able to solve that. So the instruments for this dispute settlement should get stronger.

And the third one is labor mobility. I fully agree with Carla; there was no way that would have been accepted by the US Congress. Actually, we used to say we wanted to export merchandise and not people, and that's why we were justifying why we didn't have a labor mobility or migration issue in NAFTA. Now I think it's time to think about that as well. The next three relevant issues for NAFTA are energy, labor mobility, and logistics.

Wilson: I have three, and a fourth is a throwaway. One is border management. We saw this after 9/11, that really complicated the relationship not just in those early days after 9/11 when the border just seized up. But with the impact of 9/11 it led to a number of actions taken by the United States to hurt the normal flow of traffic—different from the trucking problem.

The second thing I tried to get into both the FTA and NAFTA was dairy and poultry. We just couldn't get them to move that far. Now that's going to come, whether it's with the European deal or the TPP. I think that we'll see that change.

The third area is more our response. I was saying at the time that once we saw a greater degree of confidence with Canadian exporters being able to deal in the US market that they would naturally extend their wings and be more active in other parts of the world. Our exports to the United States are still, I think, just short of 75 percent. They reached 89 percent at a peak after the FTA. I'm not saying this as we want to diminish our relationship with the United States or with Mexico, but to expand. I think it's been too slow both ways between Canada and Mexico. As John Crosbie said, "There's too much Bush and Hills between Mexico and Canada."

Serra Puche: The statistics of trade between Canada and Mexico are complicated because many of our exports to Canada go through the US, and they classify it as a Mexico-US export. And the same for the Canadians. So we need to work something out there.

Wilson: The one thing I wish had not happened in the NAFTA negotiations was when we were in the fifth inning of the baseball game in Baltimore. Jaime wanted to get back to the negotiation. The rest of us wanted to enjoy the ballgame. As we were walking out, there's a huge roar, and it was a triple play. That's the only triple play I would have ever seen in my life.

Hills: We went to the ballgame because Michael left the negotiating table abruptly and obviously upset. I said to my staff, "The heat's getting too much. We need the night off. Where can I take them?" I suggested the Kennedy Center and said, "Get me three tickets. Maybe the President's Box is open." They found out that the Kennedy Center was dark. I said, "Where do you take two guys?" The answer was, to the ballgame. I said, "Okay, I'll do anything for my country." So we go up to Baltimore to see this game. Jaime was in the car with me. Jaime was a great soccer player; he might have been a soccer champ instead of an economist, but he definitely wasn't enthusiastic about baseball. Michael was a real fan, but he's the one who slammed out of the meeting. We could see him walking around the hotel looking very grim. So I felt the game was a good choice. We get to the game, and at about the second inning, Jaime said, "Is it time to go home yet?" I said, "We haven't had our dinner yet." Third inning. "We've had dinner; is it time?" I said, "Dessert is coming." Finally, about the sixth inning, at what I thought was the magic moment, I said, "Michael, do you think we could go back?" He said, reluctantly, "All right." And we're just getting out of the box into the hall where we cannot see the field, and there is an explosion of applause. What happened? There was the triple play. I've never heard the end of that from Michael.

Serra Puche: Sorry about that.

Taylor: On the question about how wide open the scope of agreement should be, you mentioned immigration, for example. I worry that if it gets too big, you're going to hold back the agreement. When you do these negotiations, you have your export interests and your import competing interests, and they have to work out the politics, which is going to be the more forceful in terms of putting together the package. Exporters like to have tariffs reduced abroad. And they're going to be the ones who work against your import competing firms who don't want the tariffs reduced. That's what bilateral and multilateral negotiations are all about. Otherwise you'd just reduce your barriers yourself, unilaterally. As an economist, it's very strange because we would all be better off if we just all reduced our tariffs. But, of course, that's not the politics. We will reduce our tariff if you reduce your tariff in this area. So that's why the negotiation works. That has to be chosen pretty carefully if you're going to get the right political balance. It's in addition to making these cases to the broad public. You basically have to count who's going to be the most effective lobbyist. But it seems to me that if you open this up very broadly, you're going to lose that balance. Immigration is such a big, complicated issue to bring into a trade agreement. I'm of the view that a narrower type of agreement is more likely to be successful. Yes, you want intellectual property. Yes, you want to do nontariff trade barriers. But it gets too big when it gets into other areas which are not related to trade at all.

Serra Puche: I agree with you when I say that for the future of NAFTA, labor mobility and immigration are relevant issues. However, I don't mean to change NAFTA. I mean to improve the North American region's competitiveness.

Hills: I agree that you can make an agreement too big, cover too many subjects. I don't think that in NAFTA we could have had labor mobility. But think of today, when services make up so much of our productivity as an economy. One way to prevent the initiation of cross-border services—whether it be banking or insurance—is when you can't get your people into the market. And you can't get your experts in. And so a country or a government could agree to a services opening but preclude you indirectly. That's something we're going to have to think about in the future. Also, had we been wise and able enough politically to have labor mobility, it would have actually benefited the US economy.

Taylor: Absolutely. It's a matter of what you can do—whether you may have lost NAFTA completely.

Lorenzo Caliendo: One way in which firms actually improve their productivity is by the way they organize their production and the type of employees they are able to hire. Exporters also gain in terms of productivity because they're forced to actually reorganize their production. They're receiving more competition, and because of that they have to change the type of employees they have, so any types of restriction in the labor market are going to stop those potential gains in productivity.

Wilson: One of the biggest challenges that we have right now is in terms of broadening on the regulatory or the standard-setting side. When we look at some of the issues that we have in accessing the marketplace, those are far more important now than any tariff differences.

Boskin: Increasingly, where global supply chains have become more important, the constituency for tariff reduction in a country includes importers of intermediate products. So companies like the Gap are in your office saying that they want to be able to import textiles with more liberal quotas, reduce tariffs, etc. But it's also what the value-added component is in different places. The WTO (World Trade Organization) and OECD (Organisation for Economic Co-operation and Development) have an early-stage project trying to get value-added trade accounts. It's not an easy thing to do, but in some sense that's the kind of information we really need.

The descriptions of Mexico that Steve portrayed prior to NAFTA, and Dan, to not as dramatic an extent, in Canada—the lack of competition and openness and so on—could be extended to a lot of other places. There are some other places in our hemisphere whose profile today looks not dissimilar to how you described Mexico's: roaring inflation, all of these restrictions, government nationalization of business. Pedro Aspe[7] once told me that the Mexican government owned nineteen cantinas. The politics in Argentina, Venezuela, etc., are not quite as ready for opening up as perhaps Mexico was when President Salinas came to office, but it shows how to think about some ways those places could actually do much better and maybe get to a better economic and political equilibrium.

---

7. Mexican economist; secretary of finance in the Salinas administration.

Chapter Three

The New North America

Former secretary of state George Shultz describes how NAFTA's precedent for multinational cooperation should guide North America as its residents and leaders tackle four major challenges in the near future: changing demographics and an aging population; shortcomings in K–12 educational quality; costs and violence associated with illegal drugs; and governance in an age of diversity.

Presenter: George P. Shultz
Comments: Caroline Freund, Michael H. Wilson, Michael J. Boskin, Jaime Serra Puche, Mary O'Grady, Carla A. Hills, Brian Lippey

George P. Shultz: NAFTA is really a huge achievement, with big-time implications and lots ahead. And I can't thank the people who negotiated it enough for what they did. It was very difficult, but it was done with a great deal of skill and enthusiasm. You can't work that hard unless you're enthusiastic about what you're doing.

I would like to discuss three things. First, the history as I experienced it, not involvement in the national process as such, but all around it; second, some of the immediate results; and third, what's ahead. What are the things that we need to look for and do as we go forward? We've had nine meetings now of the North American Forum, pulling together people and ideas. It has struck me how, as we've gone through this process, there has been a coalescence around the idea of North America.

First, the history. When I was secretary of the Treasury and the international monetary system was in turmoil, the finance minister of Canada, John Turner, and I worked together on the idea that we were representing our continent, North America. Mexico was not yet in the game. Then I came back to it later with President Reagan. I was his economic adviser during the primaries, the campaign, and the first part of his presidency before I became secretary of state. He was a Hoover honorary fellow and had been in residence here.

I had a dinner for him with several economists—Milton Friedman, Michael Boskin, and others—at my Stanford home before his election. He had views about a lot of things, and one of them was a vision of North America. He thought that, somehow or other, this should be in our future. At the time we had a very strong relationship with Canada and eventually negotiated the Canada free trade agreement. And Reagan felt it was clearly a prelude. I felt, as did he, that foreign policy starts in your neighborhood. We had the Cold War, China, the Middle East, and other key issues; but nevertheless, where you live is very important. So I deliberately made my first trip out of the country as secretary of state to Canada and the second trip to Mexico to make that point. I must say that the press was mystified, uninformed about the nature of our relationship; it was surprising to me.

And then I dealt with President Miguel de la Madrid. He's something of an unsung hero of a lot of what's happened. I remember him telling me, "You can't believe what the government of Mexico owns; every time somebody goes bankrupt, the government takes it over." He said, "We own beauty parlors. We own shopping malls. We own all this stuff. What are we doing? We've got to get out of this nonsense." And it was de la Madrid who put Mexico into GATT. That was a big step in 1986. So I thought de la Madrid did a lot. Then, of course, came President Salinas and Finance Minister Pedro Aspe, a different crew who had a different outlook, and we got NAFTA. That was a huge event.

I believe there has emerged out of this a sense that there is such a thing as North America. There is regional representation that's arrived without people understanding that it's happened.

The trade is gigantic. We are each other's largest trading partners. The interesting thing to me about the trade is how interconnected it is. Forty percent of the US imports from Mexico are of US origin.

Think of that. It's 25 percent from Canada. With China, by contrast, it's 4 percent. So there is an integration in trade. There are something like 230 million people a year—Canadians, Americans, Mexicans—who are in each other's countries legally. The most crossed border in the world is the US-Mexican border.

Since NAFTA, each of the three countries has negotiated free trade agreements with other countries. The number of countries that adds up to now is about fifty. Mexico has a free trade agreement with Europe. Canada has almost finalized one, and we're at least getting going on one. And what this does, in a subtle way, is expand the scope of NAFTA beyond its confines, while NAFTA and North America are the base on which this is happening. So it's a big deal. My contention, my hope, and my belief is that it can develop and continue if we do it right.

What are the problems ahead that we need to pay attention to, and the opportunities? First of all, Mexico is changing. Figure 3.1 shows that fertility in Mexico has dropped very sharply. It is now below replacement levels. What does that mean? That means that the huge numbers of young Mexicans who used to come across the border aren't coming anymore; the numbers are diminishing greatly. Combine that, particularly if the energy initiative goes forward, with the improved health of the Mexican economy. We don't have an immigration problem from Mexico anymore. Actually, the net immigration of Mexicans to the US last year was zero. I think more US citizens went to Mexico than the other way around. So it's a totally different situation.

It follows that, in our immigration debate, we're worrying about the wrong border. We should want to turn the US-Mexico border into something like what we have with Canada. While it has a little more stress than before 9/11, this has been worked on, and it has worked pretty well. You can't get by with a driver's license anymore, but a passport will do. We should do the same thing with Mexico and have a situation where people of the three countries can be in the other country, live there, not a big deal. I've tried to verify this figure, it's very big, but the San Francisco Canadian consul general says that there are a million Canadians living in California. So what? It's not an issue. If we can create a situation where people move to where they are

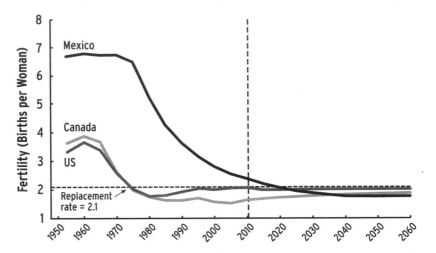

Figure 3.1 Fertility rates for the NAFTA countries. Mexico's fertility rate dropped sharply beginning in 1975 and continues to decline. Both Canada and the United States have below-replacement fertility.

Source: United Nations, "World Population Prospects 2012 Revision," medium variant forecast.

productive and fruitful and have jobs and find life good, why not? It's something we should achieve. The facts underlying the demographic situation give that opportunity a chance.

But does that mean there's not a problem on the Mexican border? There is. The problem is the southern border of North America, Mexico's southern border. And we want to help Mexico avoid becoming a transit country with all of the corruption and human degradation that goes with human trafficking. That's where the immigration issue needs to be focused. In terms of looking ahead, there is an opportunity borne out by the demographics, if nothing else.

Number two, to the extent that we think of ourselves as having a North American labor force, the evidence is very clear that the quality of your labor and the rate of growth of your GDP go right together. There are other factors; it's not just one factor. But in California, our education system is poor. Forty-three percent of the Mexican Latinos in California, who are our largest ethnic group now, don't finish high school. Only about 12 percent finish college. That's our future labor force. They have got to be able to do the jobs that are being produced by the Silicon Valley hotshots. We're failing. The problem of the distribution of income starts, in the United States, with K–12 education. Canada does a really good job in this respect; maybe they've got something to teach us. Mexico is even worse than the US so Mexico has a lot of very important work to do. And, as I interpreted it, the first thing the new president of Mexico, (Enrique) Peña Nieto, did was throw the head of the teachers' union in jail, for good reasons. There have been riots in Mexico City but the government has stood up to them. It's very encouraging and signals that there is going to be a serious effort to tackle K–12 education issues. In the United States, as in Mexico, the big problems are the teachers' unions and their influence on the Democratic Party. We're getting there; choice is developing more and more, but K–12 education is the big issue for us to face.

The third issue is drugs. And here, the culprit is the United States. Our big demand for illicit drugs and the criminalization of every aspect of it create the biggest profit margin of any industry in the world. And the industry, by definition, is criminal. The money winds up going south of our border to Mexico and Central America, and it corrupts. It makes the process of governing hard, because often the drug gangs have more money, more access to arms (which they buy in the United States, incidentally) than the local government does. As a result, we've seen huge numbers of murders—fifty thousand estimated in the last five or six years. It also results in growing addiction in the countries that are sending the drugs; the people who have this property want to develop the business, so they get kids hooked and then turn them into mules, and so on. During Prohibition, we had an amendment prohibiting alcohol; in eleven years, by a constitutional amendment, we ended it. One reason we stopped was that the violence was here in the United States: Al Capone, the Saint Valentine's Day Massacre, and so on. We have outsourced the violence, in the case of drugs, although it will come here more. This is something that we need to get after. It's not mysterious, conceptually, to know how to do it. I've backed off of the idea of legalization; that's too much for people. But I think decriminalization of the taking of drugs and small-scale possession could make a huge change. If you do that, it's possible for somebody to go to a treatment center without the risk of going to jail. Our jails are full of young kids, heavily minority. Why are they there? They got caught taking drugs and possessing a few drugs. And what do they do in jail? They learn how to be real criminals. It's a vicious cycle.

If those kids instead went to treatment centers, the evidence that we have from Portugal is that you don't get very far with the older addicts, but with young people you can make a dent, and that's worth doing! But, in the process, you take a lot of the money out of the system for the criminals. And we can begin to see a better situation in our neighborhood. The drug problem, and it's a US problem, has imposed tremendous costs on our neighbors, particularly to the south, and we should do something about it.

I had a history on this. When I left the job of secretary of state, I came back here to Stanford and I gave a talk at a Stanford alumni function. I expressed these views, and the next Monday they wound up in the *Wall Street Journal*. I never had so much mail about anything; I was inundated. Ninety-nine percent of the people who wrote said that they agreed with me, but 99 percent of them said that they would never say anything like that because they'd be afraid of being ostracized.

But since that time, things have gradually loosened up. There is a global group[1] working on this. It's not an accident that the co-chairs are three former presidents of Latin American countries: Mexico, Brazil, and Colombia. So we have an incipient rebellion if we are not careful as we look at this issue. There are ways of addressing it that would be much better for the people taking drugs and much better for society. People complain that we'd have to finance treatment centers. Of course, but that's nothing compared with the huge sums of money being poured out in the criminalization that is the war on drugs.

Number four is the problem of governance. The nations of NAFTA, the emerging North American region, show a combined GDP of about $17 trillion (figure 3.2). Our combined exports and imports are huge. The GDP of the three countries is one-quarter of the world's GDP, so we're talking about a large part of the world economy. How do we

---

1. Global Commission on Drug Policy.

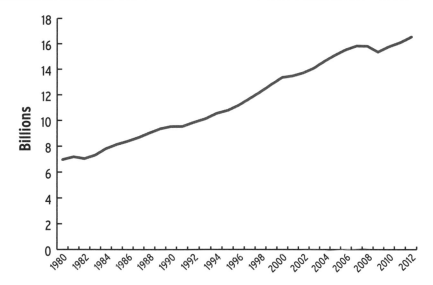

Figure 3.2 GDP of NAFTA countries, 1980–2012 (constant 2005 US$).

Source: Data from World Bank, "World Development Indicators."

govern it? How do we make it work? I have a project that I'm working on. I'm asking myself, as I look around at the great governing issues of our times on a global basis: how do you govern over diversity in an age of transparency? Diversity is everywhere, but before, it's been possible to ignore it or suppress it. You can't do that anymore because of the depth of the information and communication age. People everywhere know what's going on; they all have cellphones, they can all communicate with each other, they can organize. That hasn't been true before, but it's true now.

Take the Ukraine right now. Its leader (Viktor Yanukovych) makes a corrupt deal with (Russian president Vladimir) Putin; everybody knows it, and they know it's a bad deal for them. And he's having a hard time—he may not survive. I hope he doesn't; but at any rate, you see this everywhere. It isn't only the Arab Spring, but Brazil, Turkey, even Sweden! I recently said to a Swedish friend, "Come on, Sweden?" and she said, "It wasn't among us Swedes; we have all of these immigrants who have come into our country." I said, "All these years, you've been governing over homogeneity. Now you have diversity on your hands, and you haven't thought about how you're going to handle the diversity." I think the idea of governing over diversity is going to mean more decentralization and more ability to let diverse elements express themselves if you can keep it in some kind of common framework. And, in a way, this is the magic of North America.

That has just happened, with NAFTA as the key. Nobody's bossing anybody around. Compare it with Europe. In Europe, you have a national government, but a big chunk of your sovereignty has been given away to Brussels. Another big chunk has been given away to Frankfurt. So it's no wonder they're having trouble. In the case of NAFTA, with the exception of the trade agreement itself, nobody's sovereignty is being affected at all. You run your country the way you want to run your country. And I think that it's very important, as we project NAFTA forward, to keep it that way. Resist the temptation to say, "Let's create something or other that's going to run this or that or the other thing," though obviously you have to have agreements on certain things like immigration and the border.

It's interesting to look at the history of the United States in this regard. Our founding fathers understood that they had thirteen very different states on their hands, and if they didn't recognize that in the Constitution, they'd never get it ratified. So they designed a form of government that had never existed before. They projected a federal government with limited powers, so that practically everything that affected daily life was left in the hands of the states, the localities, and individuals. And in the federal government the powers were checked and balanced among the legislative, executive, and judicial branches. But within the legislative branch, they designed two very different bodies.

The House of Representatives was designed to represent the population by numbers, and it operates by majority vote. The Senate was totally different in conception. Each state had two senators, which meant that small states were represented as strongly as big states, so big states couldn't push them around. It's written into the Constitution that on several things, like treaty ratification, you've got to have a two-thirds vote. The convention in early times was that anything important took place on a two-thirds vote. Why? Because they wanted to encourage discussion back and forth and come to an agreement. That is why the Senate was described in earlier days as the greatest deliberative body in the world. We recently have junked that, unfortunately. It's a big change. The federal government has also gradually moved in on state and local purviews in a way that is breathtaking.

And the new health law, where the federal government tells a twenty-five-year-old kid that he has to buy something he doesn't want to buy? Wow! What would our framers have thought of that? So we have some thinking to do. Actually, I think we're going to have a rebellion among young people one of these days because they're more and more saying that the system is rigged to favor older people. That's just one example, but you can think of many examples where it looks as though the system is rigged against young people. Climate change: I'm ninety-three years old—who cares? But I have four great-grandchildren. I look at these little kids, the oldest is a little over three, and the others around one or so, and I think to myself, what kind of a world are they going to inherit? What can I do to make it a bit better? People say the climate isn't changing. Are you kidding? We're probably not going to feel it much, but forty or fifty years from now?

I think the fact that North America has emerged in its own terms, a natural reaction to the opportunity put there, is the right way to govern it. But the minute somebody decides we ought to have some overall framework, no! Stay away from that, and let the diversity express itself as it's been doing. Then we will have a North America that really works well. I think that you people who put it together have a right to be a bit proud of yourselves, because you have created something that, as Stephen says, goes far beyond trade. It's created something different that can be very good and positive for people in all countries.

Caroline Freund: You mentioned the drug trade and the changes there. I was just curious about your views on the other side of the drug trade, which is the guns trade.

Shultz: Well, they are part and parcel. Practically all the guns that the drug lords use are bought in the United States, which is another problem. But the basic problem is that, by the criminalization of drugs, we've created this profit spread. Any business that would have a spread like this is hugely profitable. And it's all criminalized, so they buy guns. They buy whatever they want. And they say to local officials, so I'm told, "What do you want? Silver or lead? A bribe or a bullet?" And they get their way. So it's a very unholy problem.

Way back forty years ago, when this started, I was director of the budget. My friend, Pat Moynihan, was in the White House and he became a kind of self-appointed drug czar. He had the idea that the way to curtail drug use in this country was to keep drugs out of the country, so that's what he was busy doing. The two of us were riding to Camp David. I had a presentation to make, so I was busy studying, getting ready, but he was in a state of exuberance. An Irishman in a state of exuberance is something else. So he started, "Hey, Shultz! We just had the biggest drug bust in history!" I said, "Great work!" Back to my notes. "Come on, this was in Marseilles! We've broken the French connection!" (That was the problem of the day.) I said, "That's great, Pat." He was very frustrated. There was a pause, and he said, "Shultz, I suppose you think that, as long as there's a large, profitable demand for drugs in this country, there will be a supply." I said, "Moynihan, there's hope for you."

Drugs are plentiful in this country. We aren't successful in curbing the use of drugs, because we don't try to treat them in any sensible way. We just say, "You're a criminal if you take them, and that's that." That's not enough.

Mary O'Grady: On that subject, maybe I shouldn't say this, since there are so many people in here who have worked in Washington, but it seems to me that the likelihood of getting change from Washington on this issue is very low because of incentives, interests, and so forth. Do you think that we're seeing, right now, a grass-roots interest in change, coming from states, regarding marijuana? Do you think there might be another way we could get at the problem that would be more effective than trying to get Washington to lead on it?

Shultz: That's where the only action is, in states. I'm antsy about what's going on in the states because these votes on marijuana are more-or-less saying marijuana is OK. I don't think it's OK. I'd like to see anything done to decriminalize marijuana, fine. But couple it with a health initiative so that we're saying, at the same time, "Let's get people not to take these drugs." Let's approach it the same as we try to get people not to get drunk. I think "driving under the influence" should absolutely apply to anybody having drugs, for example. There are states where people are doing something and, at least at this point, the federal government is laying off. When California started, there were threats to preempt this. But they're laying off right now.

Michael H. Wilson: Could I just ask a broader question, George? This question of North America—I'm part of the North American Forum. We have good discussions there, but the sense that I've had is that in Washington, whether there's too much on their plate right now or whatever, the desire to look at the region as a North American region does not have any real support. Would you agree with that? And, if you do, what can be done to get the United States to broaden its perspective? I raised the question of a North American region at the trilateral,[2] about a year-and-a-half ago, and I got a very good response from the Mexicans, but the Americans said, "No, don't push that idea."

Shultz: I don't think that it's opposition. People just haven't been paying attention. One of the objectives of this North American Forum is to help bring that about. At the last meeting, we had a terrific turn-out of the Mexican government that came and talked to us, and Canada was well-represented. Unfortunately, it came during the US government shutdown, so we had one assistant secretary of state there but no others. We have had the chairman of the Joint Chiefs of Staff and a lot of other people. Letting people see the advantages of what we have going for us is important. It's important also to be reassuring to people, and say, "We don't have in mind any big supranational government. The whole idea of governance of North America is to create

---

2. The North American Leaders Summit is an annual meeting by the leaders of Canada, Mexico, and the United States, commonly referred to as the trilateral summit.

conditions where people do what comes naturally to them. Don't try to govern it, or have somebody tell you what you're supposed to do."

Michael Boskin: This in part obviously depends on attitudes of leaders and what they're confronting. In the early spring, 1989, in discussions in the (White House) Situation Room about Brady Bonds, it was clear that the Latin Americans wanted debt reduction, but our banks were adamant against it because they would have to take large write-downs. The main Treasury negotiator, David Mulford, pushed hard for debt reduction. The Fed was wary. Then President Bush made it very clear he wanted to do something for the region, especially for Mexico, to let them know they were our friend and partner, which would help change attitudes in Mexico and be good for us and for those trying to reform the Mexican economy. President Bush was very explicit that this was his main concern. And that's when I initially raised the idea of trade liberalization with Mexico, although nothing as well-thought-out as a full-scale FTA.

Shultz: Boy, does leadership matter! That's one lesson I've learned.

Jaime Serra Puche: I have the feeling, and usually it's shared by other foreigners, that the agenda in the US State Department is usually a sort of adverse selection of issues. When there is complication and trouble, foreign affairs go up in the agenda very quickly. And when things are working out, international issues go naturally down in the agenda. So as a Mexican, I sense (I don't know if the Canadians have the same feeling) that the US takes us for granted.

Shultz: When I was in office, I talked about that a lot with others like Henry Kissinger. In the US, we have to conduct a global diplomacy. We don't want to pivot here or pivot there. We've got to have an ability to be effective everywhere. Then, within that framework, have a strategy, and I say: start with your neighborhood. That's where you live. When you buy a house, you look at the house but also the neighborhood: are the schools any good, and so on. Looking after your neighborhood is just common sense.

Carla A. Hills: I think that the North American Forum is a great idea, George. Also, your concept of not thinking about ourselves separately as Canada, Mexico, and the United States, but as the North American region, and for the reasons that you articulated, which included how to get things on the agenda, and how to deal with the separation of powers. I think that the reason Michael got that answer of US indifference at the trilateral meeting is that the people he was talking with were uninformed.

There has been a movement by a few to have a North American Customs Union. I've always opposed that. I think that's a step too far. If you begin to tell the respective governments how they should govern themselves, you're going to get a pushback. I think that we could sell the Shultz idea, but you have to start somewhere, and that is by telling business organizations, universities, think tanks, and the like what we mean when we talk about a North American Forum and what are its advantages. Why do we want to do this?

You asked the question about guns. It appalls me that we had legislated a ban on assault weapons going to Mexico that expired in 2004. Well, if it was a good idea in 2003, why don't we have it in 2013? This is crazy that we cannot educate people about this kind of issue. Nobody's really picked it up and tried to sell the notion of why it is we need to control this area. So, I think it's an educational effort, and I have such admiration for what you've done in this sphere.

Shultz: We should meld a North American effort, a task force or other body, to develop ideas, keep track, and be a center of work and research on the subject.

Boskin: It's a natural, there's no doubt about that. When something is successful, people tend to imitate it; so, for example, there is a SAFTA,[3] a South Asian free trade agreement. It hasn't worked all that well. It's among the Pakistanis, Indians, Bangladeshis, Sri Lankans, Nepalese, Bhutanese, Maldivians, etc. And so the Indians have gone

---

3. South Asian Free Trade Agreement.

ahead and signed bilateral FTAs with Bangladesh and Sri Lanka, and the Pakistanis are left out in the cold.

There's been too little tariff reduction. There's a very large negative list. There's not a serious positive list, so Pakistan exports a lot more to Bangladesh (some of which undoubtedly goes back into India) than it does to nearby and vastly larger India, which is nonsense. George and Bill Perry[4] have a group that tries to work on a Track II basis with the Indians and Pakistanis. One of the points that your neighborhood idea drives home to me is that, if you draw a circle around India, it goes through virtually every tough patch in the world. Yet there's democracy in India. They have an immense state, and people in those other societies have a huge stake in their success and vice versa. So there's been a little progress on some slight trade openings. But I think this neighborhood idea is central to unlocking one of the great difficulties in world affairs and, very clearly, nuclear dangers.

Shultz: We had the Indians and Pakistanis here, retired generals and foreign ministers, people who still had influence but weren't actually in the government. They were focusing more on nuclear things, but we suggested that somebody make a calculation of how much it is costing Pakistan not to have any reasonable amount of trade with India. How much could their GDP and income per capita increase? It's a large number. And I got word the other day that one of the people there had taken that up and had produced an estimate. Now he wants to bring it here, and we should welcome him.

Boskin: A simple gravity model, the basic economic model predicting bilateral trade flows, would predict that Pakistan would export between twenty-five and fifty times as much to India as it does. That's potentially a huge gain for both countries.

Hills: When you write your report, you should take note of the fact that United States' tariffs, although relatively low on average, on products coming from the poorest countries in the world are enormously

---

4. William Perry was secretary of defense in the Clinton administration.

high. We charge Bangladesh sixteen times more for its exports to us than we charge Great Britain and, in fact, Bangladesh pays us more in tariffs to cover miniscule amounts of export than does Britain on huge exports. I can send you the figures, and it is not just Bangladesh, but Pakistan, Indonesia—the largest Muslim countries in the world pay us multiples of what Western countries pay us in tariffs. We still have Smoot-Hawley tariffs on the products that poor countries make, like cheap shoes, heavy glass, textiles, and apparel.

Boskin: That's a great point, and it follows the issues Jaime was discussing about data. A great project would be a model of what the effective tariffs are in all of these relations; you could "tariffize" the quotas, adjust for rules of origin, and that would indicate where the largest potential gains from trade liberalization would be.

Wilson: What are the benefits of thinking of us as a North American region, whether it's in trade, energy, or a range of other issues? We've got to somehow get the leadership of the three countries to take it as a priority. Picking up on your comment on leadership, George, how can they lead their countries into thinking of the North American concept so that it conveys to the business community, the academic community, the union community, and others that the world is bigger than each of our countries, and if we can act in a concerted way there will be significant benefits that we're not achieving now?

Boskin: Let me ask a demography question. You have these charts about Mexico and the US and Canada, but comparing Mexico to China as a developing country where the population is going to age rapidly, and Mexico will be as old or older than America, as will China in a generation or so. When I've discussed various reforms with the Chinese, I've continually made the case that you need to get rich before you get old. The biggest battle going on in the US budget is about future entitlement costs. We're worried about that in the US, but we're really rich. Still, it's a big problem here, as you were saying, about having younger people needing opportunities and the taxes they'll pay if we don't get this under control in the interim. But it's a lot easier to be rich and old than not-so-rich and old or poor and old. So Mexico in particular should be thinking a lot about this problem. Is there a generalized strategic thinking in Mexico about the economics of the aging population?

Serra Puche: Yes, in the government. First of all, we have accumulated some past problems that are very delicate: because of improperly designed pension funds, serious problems have arisen over financing people's retirement. So the government is addressing the task of adjusting our public finance. Fortunately, we have demographic capital to fix that, and we have created a forced saving mechanism for workers called AFORE.[5] These are pension funds that are regulated by financial law. And we believe that, by 2030, all those pension funds will be paying for retirements. Now this is not independent of what happens to the NAFTA demographics because there's a great deal of complementarity between demography in the US, Canada, and Mexico. The NAFTA pyramid in figure 3.3 shows that the implicit dependency ratio in Mexico is much lower than in the US and Canada. If you look at the dependency ratio applied to young people in Mexico, it's very high. The dependency ratio applied to old people is very low.

Boskin: Right now.

Serra Puche: When you contemplate the three countries together, the dependency ratios become much healthier. That's why I think the issues of migration and labor mobility become extremely relevant for the region.

Brian Lippey: I'd like to get your thoughts on one of the key constituents in all of this, and that is the labor unions and the inertia that has built up historically, resisting further integration. You mention the teachers' unions as an impediment to educational reform. How do you see this all evolving as North America continues to integrate?

---

5. Administradora de Fondos para el Retiro.

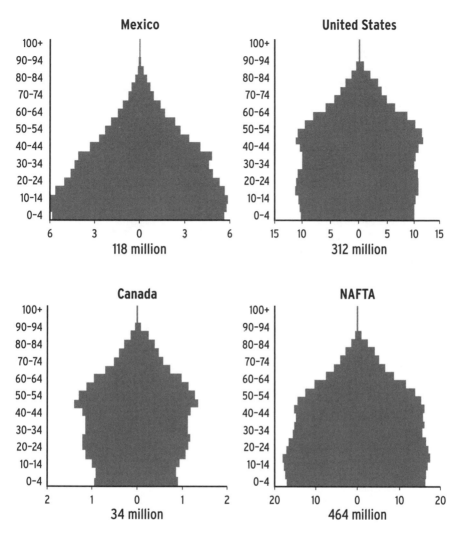

Figure 3.3 NAFTA 2010. Different shapes, different realities. Declining fertility and increasing longevity determine variation in age structure. Population by five-year age bracket in millions; males on left, females on right.

Source: United Nations, "World Population Prospects: The 2012 Revision," medium variant forecast.

Shultz: In the United States, the labor movement has changed dramatically. It used to be a private-sector labor movement. But now I think it's about half, maybe more than half, public-sector unionization, and its issues are different. If you're an auto worker, you worry about auto competition, and so on. But for public-sector unions, there aren't competitors for the US taxpayer dollar in the same sense. So I think that your teachers' union problem is not really related to North America. If you think about the labor force in North America, the quality of that labor force will stem from what we do about K–12 education.

Chapter Four

Evaluating the Effects
of NAFTA

Separating the effects of NAFTA from the effects of other events and free trade agreements is difficult, but the effect has obviously been positive for all three signatory nations, largest for Mexico, the least developed. Economists Lorenzo Caliendo and Caroline Freund quantify the treaty's effects, with special attention to tariffs.

Presenters: Lorenzo Caliendo, Caroline Freund
Comments: Kyle Bagwell, Michael J. Boskin, Jaime Serra Puche, Daniel Trefler, Michael H. Wilson, Diego Perez, Mary O'Grady, Alan Sykes

Kyle Bagwell: In evaluating the effects of NAFTA, our speakers will focus principally on its economic effects. When you think about it, you can quickly identify several considerations that you would like to assess. First, you would want to know what are the effects of NAFTA on member countries. In particular, to what extent did it contribute to increases in trade? Maybe even more ambitiously, to what extent did it change welfare, and can we put numbers to that? Second, you might also want to know what was the effect of NAFTA on nonmember countries; in particular, to what extent might there have been trade diversion that came about through NAFTA?

A third thing that might be of interest would be the broader effects of NAFTA on trade liberalization, something that I know Caroline will talk about: the effects on external tariffs of member countries. Might regional agreements be catalysts for other rounds of negotiation multilaterally or for other regional agreements?

There are a lot of things to think about. Fortunately, we have two experts who can guide us through these considerations. We will start with Lorenzo Caliendo, who is coming to us from Yale.

Lorenzo Caliendo: I am going to talk about the economic effects of NAFTA. These are results of the research that I have ongoing with Fernando Parro, who is an economist at the Federal Reserve Board. I want to answer three questions: Why was NAFTA different compared to any other agreement? Why is it difficult to measure the economic effects of NAFTA in general? And then, quantifying the economic effects of NAFTA, I am going to focus on tariff reductions and the effect that had on trade flows, wages, and welfare.

Why was NAFTA different? NAFTA was different because it was among members that were in very different stages of development. Figure 4.1 shows the sizes of FTAs in force by the year 1995 in terms of shared GDP in the world. You can see that NAFTA was the largest one when it was signed. This is the agreement that would have the most resources in the world involved. Of course, each time the US signs an agreement, this would always happen, but back then, it was one of the first.

Why it was particularly different is also because it was an agreement between very different countries in terms of their GDP per capita. The GDP per capita of Mexico back then was one-fifth the US level. Looking at the inequality across members for different types of agreements prior to 1995, NAFTA was among the most unequal agreements, and one of the largest.

When countries are in very different stages of development, they trade different types of goods. Figure 4.2 shows Mexican imports from NAFTA members and from the rest of the world, US imports, and Canadian imports, divided by different types of goods. These include final goods, which are usually thought of as goods for consumption; intermediate goods, which are basically processed materials; and raw materials.

The first thing you notice is that most trade happens in processed material—intermediate goods. This was true before NAFTA, in 1993. That is the first observation. Second is that this was particularly

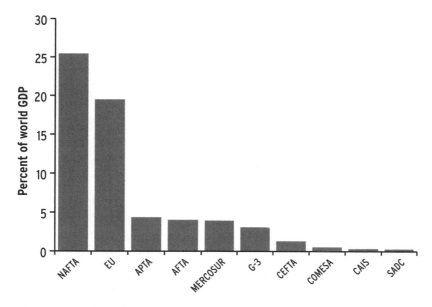

Figure 4.1 Size of FTAs in force by 1995.

Source: Data from World Trade Organization and World Bank, "World Development Indicators."

important for NAFTA. These countries were importing processed materials—intermediate goods—much more between each other than they were importing from the rest of the world. This builds on the idea that Michael Wilson has mentioned, that it is North America's supply chain. They were trading a lot of intermediate goods.

In particular, how is it different in Mexico compared to Canada and the US? Mexico imported many more intermediate goods from Canada and the US than the US and Canada imported from Mexico. Eighty percent of imports to Mexico were intermediate goods.

But if you look at the US and Canada, what did they do? They mostly imported intermediate goods, but there was a larger share of final goods. You have a country like Mexico supplying final goods to the US and Canada. Canada and the US are supplying intermediate goods to Mexico.

My first point is that an assessment of the economic effects of NAFTA has to take into account two things: (1) that these countries are in very different stages of development, and therefore produce

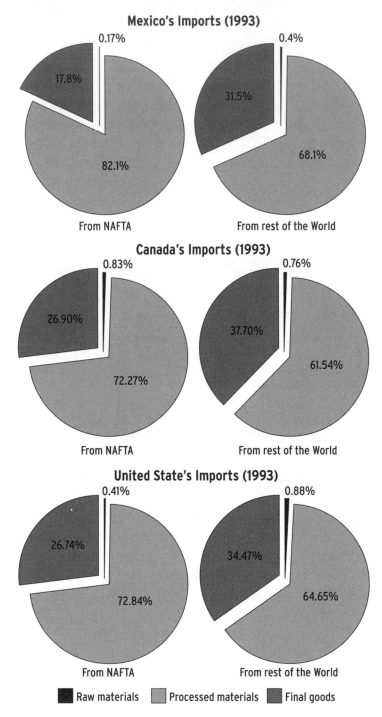

Figure 4.2 What goods were they trading?
Source: Data from World Bank's World Integrated Trade Solution.

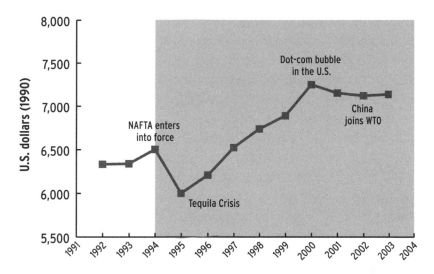

Figure 4.3 GDP per capita of Mexico.
Source: Data from Angus Maddison data set; see http://www.ggdc.net/maddison.

different goods; and (2) that most of the trade, if it is going to have an economic effect, has to be via intermediate goods. That is bottom line number one.

Bottom line number two is that it is very difficult to measure the economic effects of NAFTA because it is difficult to identify the NAFTA effect. Figure 4.3 shows Mexico's GDP per capita over time. In 1995, what happened? The Tequila Crisis[1] in Mexico. There was a big reduction in GDP per capita. There was a big—more than 40 percent—increase in inflation in Mexico, also unemployment and other issues. Over time, there was the dot-com bubble in the US in 2000, and then China joined the WTO. Many things happened after NAFTA which, in a way, contaminate any possible analysis to actually identify the effects of NAFTA.

Not only that, after NAFTA, these countries started signing free trade agreements with many other countries. By 2006, Mexico had signed more than ten free trade agreements—even more since then.

---

1. The Tequila Crisis was an economic downturn caused by sudden devaluation of the peso in December 1994.

This is a challenge. How do you identify the effects of NAFTA when so many other things were happening at the same time . . . external events that these countries were exposed to, not directly related to NAFTA, like the Tequila Crisis, the dot-com bubble and China's accession to the WTO? And after NAFTA, these countries signed several free trade agreements.

In an attempt to quantify the economic effects of NAFTA's tariff reduction, I am going to focus only on the effects of NAFTA in the case of tariff reduction. Carla made the point that tariff reduction was the major policy of NAFTA. I will focus on NAFTA, not the Canada-US Free Trade Agreement. I am going to build on academic work that actually tries to incorporate these channels. We have multiple countries that trade very different goods, most of them intermediate goods. New methodologies allow us to isolate the pure effects of tariff changes. I will build on new methodologies in international trade to incorporate those channels, which I believe are important for NAFTA, and try to say something about the North American Free Trade Agreement and, in particular, the effects of tariffs.

Why tariffs? What you see in figure 4.4 are applied tariffs from different countries, across members in 1993, before NAFTA entered into effect. There are six items. The first one is applied tariff rates from Mexico to Canada in 1993. They were mostly high and they varied across manufacturing sectors. The tariffs that Canada and the US applied between each other by 1993 were basically low, in part because the Canadian-American Free Trade Agreement[2] was already in place.

This tariff actually went to zero by the year 2005. What happens in different economies when all these tariffs that are different across sectors go to zero? What are the reallocations of resources across countries, trade effects, and welfare effects?

Figure 4.5 shows the share of total imports that Canada had from the US and Mexico before the agreement. One hundred percent will be the total imports from NAFTA members. Ninety-seven percent of those imports came from the US, while only 3 percent came from Mexico. After the change in tariffs, we find that Canada's imports from

---

2. CUSFTA, or Canada-US Free Trade Agreement.

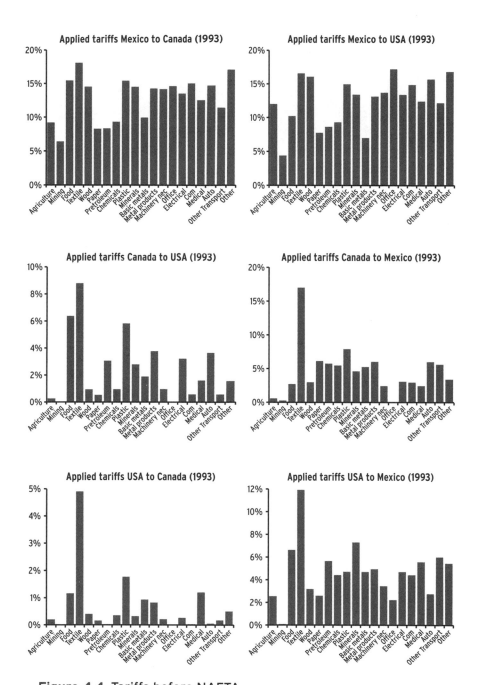

Figure 4.4 Tariffs before NAFTA.

Source: Data from World Bank's World Integrated Trade Solution.

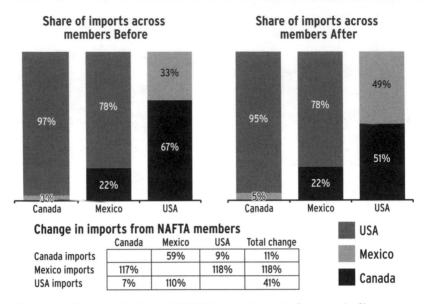

Change in imports from NAFTA members

	Canada	Mexico	USA	Total change
Canada imports		59%	9%	11%
Mexico imports	117%		118%	118%
USA imports	7%	110%		41%

Figure 4.5 Imports from NAFTA members before and after.
Source: Lorenzo Caliendo and Fernando Parro, "Estimates of the Trade and Welfare Effects of NAFTA," NBER Working Paper No. 18508, November 2012.

Mexico increased by almost 60 percent, imports from the US almost 9 percent. The change in the share of Canada's imports from these members was not so much. It was a big effect in terms of trade flows, but it did not change the composition of who you were importing from. You were mostly importing from the US.

But the effect on Mexican imports is very pronounced. Mexico's imports increased more than 117 percent from Canada and 119 percent from the US. This was a big trade effect, but it did increase proportionally across members. If you look at the share of Mexican imports from Canada and the US before and after the agreement, the share remained constant.

You see a different effect for the US. Before the agreement, the US imported one-third of its goods from Mexico, i.e., one-third of the share of goods it imported from NAFTA members was from Mexico. After the agreement, this number went to 50 percent. After the agreement, Mexico started importing many more goods from Canada and the US. Which types of goods? Intermediate goods, which are used for

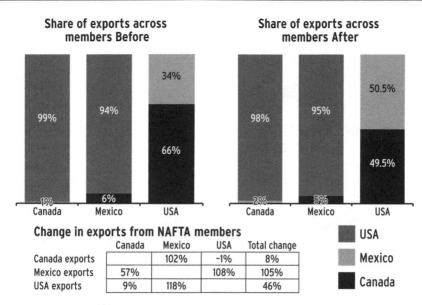

Figure 4.6 Exports from NAFTA members before and after.
Source: Lorenzo Caliendo and Fernando Parro, "Estimates of the Trade and Welfare Effects of NAFTA," NBER Working Paper No. 18508, November 2012.

production and eventually allow them to export goods. And Mexico's exports of goods to the US after the agreement went from one-third to 49 percent.

Figure 4.6 shows basically the same figures from the other side. Canada's exports to Mexico after the agreement increased 102 percent because Canada was exporting intermediate goods. Mexico's exports to Canada went up 57 percent, but its exports to the US went up 108 percent. Mexico imported intermediate goods from Canada and the US, processed these goods, then exported them back to the other members, most as final goods. Finally, the same happened for the US. The US's exports to Mexico increased 118 percent as a result of the reductions in tariffs.

Figure 4.7 shows the change in real wages. NAFTA generated a real increase in wages for all members—Mexico, Canada, and the US—but Mexico was the largest winner. There is a distinction between real income gains and welfare. You can see that most of the welfare gains actually went to Mexico. The US and Canada, in terms of welfare,

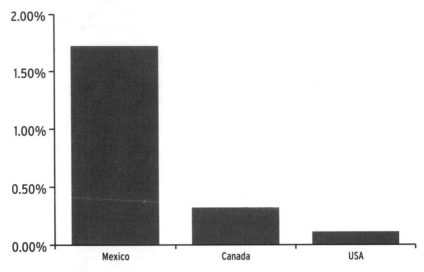

Figure 4.7 Change in real wages.
Source: Lorenzo Caliendo and Fernando Parro, "Estimates of the Trade and Welfare Effects of NAFTA," NBER Working Paper No. 18508, November 2012.

gained considerably less than Mexico. We can decompose this welfare to see where it comes from. Does it come from the fact that you were able to create more trade? Does it come from changes in the terms of trade?

The terms of trade basically reflect a country's purchasing power. It indicates how much the price of the goods that you exported has changed relative to the price of the goods that you imported. The terms of trade of Mexico and Canada deteriorated after the agreement. There was a lot of trade creation after the agreement, particularly because of the intermediate goods. Mexico had access to cheaper intermediate goods and that made it more productive. Being more productive reduced the exporter prices. This reduction in costs for Mexico implies that the exporter price of Mexico went down, due to access to cheaper intermediate goods. The volume of trade creation allowed Mexico to have a positive welfare effect.

It is important to emphasize the sectorial aspect. Textiles and electrical equipment were two sectors where more trade was created for NAFTA members. This was particularly the case for Mexico and the US. You can see it in the data. The trade creation in textiles was

6 percent for Mexico and for the US it was more than 4 percent. The effects on Canada are slightly smaller.

To summarize the results of this study, we find that NAFTA generated large trade effects, mostly because of trade in intermediate goods which are used as inputs to produce other intermediate and final goods. Real wages increased for all NAFTA members. Mexico was the largest winner in terms of welfare because of NAFTA. We find that most of the benefits obtained were through trade creation, and that by importing intermediate goods, Mexico managed to export more goods.

Caroline Freund: Conferences like these, especially with the quality of people that we have here, are just great for the research community, because we learn from policymakers to direct our research to the real issues that are most important for trade policy.

I was in graduate school when NAFTA was being negotiated. The economic research on trade agreements, regional trade agreements, free trade agreements, or preferential trade agreements has changed over this time. My first professor to talk about regional trade agreements was Jagdish Bhagwati.[3] He was the strongest proponent of free trade, but not of preferential trade agreements.

What the multilateralists like Bhagwati opposed in free trade agreements was that they could be discriminatory. Free traders or multilateralists did not like the potential for trade diversion that comes from a discriminatory trade agreement. Free traders did not like the potential stumbling block that an agreement could form if, because you have this agreement, you try to protect the borders around the free trade area. Multilateralists also did not like the rules of origin that ended up cluttering the trade system, as in the case of free trade.

The view at that time was very ambiguous on whether FTAs were a good thing. Now people view them much more as, "Whatever channel to liberalize trade is open, let's take." Overall, these second-best types of considerations have not panned out to be particularly large. Whatever channel is open is good to take.

---

3. Professor of economics and law at Columbia University.

Let's go back and consider what some of the concerns were, and then I will use some of the techniques that I have used with Emanuel Ornelas,[4] Antoni Estevadeordal,[5] and a few others to evaluate trade agreements. The main initial concern was trade diversion, static welfare losses, where you might start importing more from a less efficient producer at the expense of the production of a more efficient producer. In which case, overall, a trade agreement may not be welfare-enhancing, especially for the more efficient producer who is left out. Or even for the importer, who may still be importing some quantity of goods from outside countries, potentially leaving the prices unchanged, implying there can be a loss in tariff revenue with no gain in consumer surplus.

Diversion is going to be greater if your tariffs are high or if you form an agreement with someone who is not your natural partner, who does not produce goods that you purchase a lot of. But regional agreements are not formed at random; they are formed endogenously. The ones that have been truly successful, like NAFTA, are those formed with natural partners. If tariffs are high, there is an incentive to reduce them because of the trade agreement and to reduce the potential dangers.

The most common way to look at trade diversion is in a gravity-model approach, where we find that creation strongly dominates diversion. There are also some very specific studies of NAFTA looking at products that have been liberalized and how trade has changed with members and nonmembers. Dan has done one of those important studies on the Canada-US Free Trade Agreement and found it to be trade-creating, though Romalis,[6] in 2007, found NAFTA to be trade-diverting for Mexico. That study was done right when tariffs had gone up in Mexico, after the debt crisis; I do not think that holds anymore.

---

4. Associate professor of managerial economics and strategy, London School of Economics.

5. Manager of the integration and trade sector, Inter-American Development Bank, Washington, DC.

6. John Romalis, "NAFTA's and CUSFTA's Impact on International Trade," *Review of Economics and Statistics* 89 (3) 2007.

To the extent there is diversion or creation, external tariff reduction might reduce it. That is what I will show in the case of Mexico: that when natural partners form agreements, you do get creation.

The second concern—of stumbling blocs—is probably more pernicious. Over the long run, because of free trade agreements, you may not get to a more liberalized global economy because countries may protect the group.

There may be a political incentive to maintain external tariffs in order to protect preference margins. If you have the agreement, in order to have side commitments on things like drugs, migration, or noneconomic issues, then it may be important to maintain preference margins with your agreement partners. That would be a reason why such agreements could lead to less liberalization. However, working against this, there is an economic incentive for a country to lower its external tariffs because, as an importer, it will reduce any costly diversion.

Overall, there is no consensus, though most of the studies find that regionalism is good and that if you just look at what has happened to tariffs over time across countries and what has happened to preferences, they both tend to move together. Still, that could be the effects of broader liberalization, with regional agreements somewhat slowing it down. When we look at very specific tariff line data, we still tend to find this effect for many of the agreements, suggesting preferential liberalization supports external tariff reduction.

Let me focus on NAFTA. In 2012, there was over $1 trillion in merchandise trade, up from $300 billion in 1993. There was $123 billion in services. FDI (foreign direct investment) tripled to over $600 billion among the three countries.

In figure 4.8, we look at trade shares to get a glimpse of what might have happened from NAFTA. We do not see a steep jump up, trade shifting completely to the partners, as if the agreement had been very diverting. We see some jump up in imports in the early years, but also very clearly the emergence of China and other countries. The graph on the left shows that the share of each country's total imports coming from other NAFTA members actually falls in the 2000s as this ensues. In contrast, the share of each member's total exports that go to the other members increased and then came back to initial levels towards

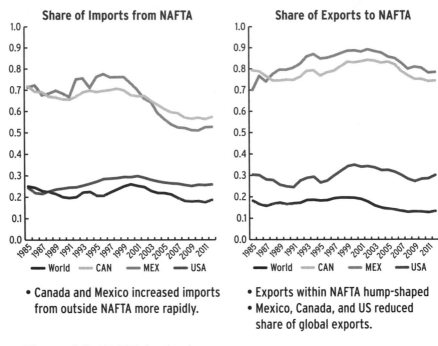

Share of Imports from NAFTA — • Canada and Mexico increased imports from outside NAFTA more rapidly.

Share of Exports to NAFTA — • Exports within NAFTA hump-shaped • Mexico, Canada, and US reduced share of global exports.

Figure 4.8 NAFTA trade shares.

Source: Data from UN Comtrade Database; see http://comtrade.un.org.

the end of the period. Importantly, the NAFTA export shares of its members remained stronger than the region's share of global exports, indicating that NAFTA markets are more important to NAFTA members than they are to the rest of the world. Overall, the strength in regional export shares shows that the agreement has been important for Canada, Mexico, and the US; but the graphs also do not suggest that there was a lot of diversion.

With so many other things going on in the world, we cannot understand what happens just by looking at aggregate figures. Over the same period, Canada reduced tariffs. Figure 4.9 shows the average MFN (most favored nation) tariff. Canada reduced tariffs quite sharply over the period, as did Mexico post the mid-2000s. The US did, but at a slower rate, starting from a lower level to begin with.

This also speaks to the Romalis study, done using data to about 2005, which found evidence of trade diversion in Mexico. He was looking precisely at the period when Mexican tariffs were at their

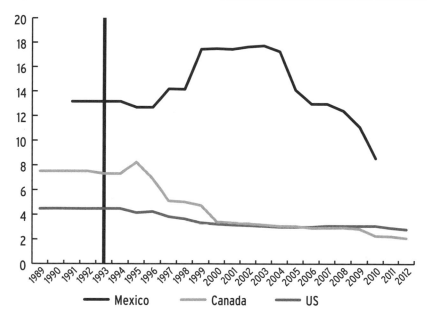

Figure 4.9 Average MFN tariffs in NAFTA.
Source: Data from UN Comtrade Database; see http://comtrade.un.org.

peak. What we have seen from the aggregate data is that trade shares did not adjust sharply to favor NAFTA. In part this is because external tariffs fell, except in the short run in Mexico. The counterfactual is unclear. What would have happened without NAFTA? How important was NAFTA in generating this picture?

Economists have turned to disaggregated data, which allows a more careful analysis. We now have twenty years of MFN tariffs, twenty years of the preferential tariffs. Since they were not immediately reduced to zero, we can look at whether NAFTA imports at the very specific product group level increased more in products where there were greater trade preferences or preference margins. We can also look at what happened to the external tariffs on those products that had the bigger margins. When you had a bigger margin in footwear, were you more likely or less likely to reduce your external tariff in footwear? When you had a big margin, what happened to imports from NAFTA members and how did that margin affect imports from nonmembers?

The advantage of this disaggregate data is that you can control for overall trends in the country, in the industry, and things that were going on otherwise, as opposed to aggregate data, where it is very difficult to deal with those issues.

Applying these techniques to NAFTA, what we find is quite interesting. Figure 4.9 shows average tariffs from 1994 to 2012. Mexico's average tariff was much higher than Canada and the US, and its average margin—the difference between the external tariff and the preferential tariff—was also much higher. The US and Canada had a much better deal to some extent in Mexico, than Mexico had in the US and Canada, from a mercantilist perspective.

How much did a one percentage point greater margin—the difference between what you charge the rest of the world and what you charge each other—generate in additional trade between the partners? For all three countries together, we get about 3 percent for one percentage point greater preference margin. We get very little diversion. The differences among the three countries are striking. In Mexico, there was both trade creation and trade diversion, though creation still far outweighed diversion. This is in part because of the higher tariffs. In Canada and the US, there was trade creation with the partner countries, but there was actually creation with nonmembers. Margins increased trade from countries outside of the union (figure 4.10).

There are two potential explanations for this. One is that other preferences were being put into place at the same time, for example, through GSP and the Central American Free Trade Agreement. There were these other agreements going on, and maybe they were correlated with the NAFTA margins. The other possibility that relates to Lorenzo's work is that it had to do with supply chains. Increasing trade in these product groups with Canada and Mexico also meant you needed more very similar types of goods from other countries, or round-tripping. This is much more likely to happen precisely when tariffs themselves are low, as they were in Canada and the US. In the case of Canada, when we really see this trade creation happening a lot, it may also have to do with the fact that it was the country where general liberalization was most strongly correlated with NAFTA liberalization.

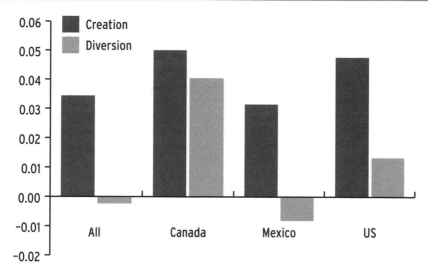

Figure 4.10 Creation and diversion.
Source: Results from analysis using UN Comtrade Database; http://see comtrade.un.org.

The second big concern is whether it is going to prevent us from moving forward on liberalization. Figure 4.11 shows the change in preferential tariffs over the whole period from 1993 to 2012 versus the change in MFN tariffs. A positive line means that when one is reduced a lot, the other is also reduced a lot over the period. That is what you can see from the pictures in most cases. In general, there certainly is not a negative trend. That is what we call tariff complementarity.

You can use the same types of panel estimates to look within a specific product. As the preference goes down, what happens next year to the MFN tariff? Again, you find this complementary relationship where preferential tariff reduction tends to encourage more MFN reduction, not less. This was especially the case in Canada, but also significant in the US and Mexico. Figure 4.12 shows that a one percentage point increase in the preference margin tends to be associated with about a one-third percentage point external tariff reduction, a reduction that benefits all MFN countries.

Michael Boskin: Hold up for a second. That one-third of a percentage point was to apply to a larger cumulative volume.

Freund: Yes.

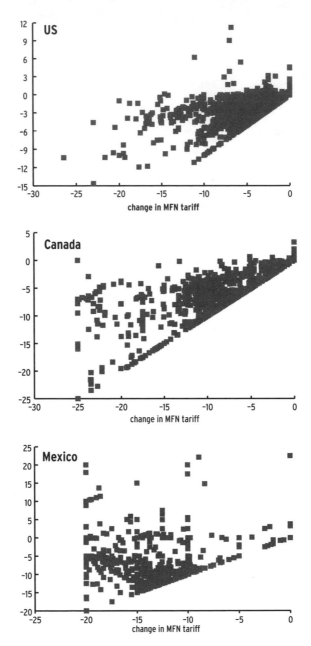

Figure 4.11 Preferential tariff reduction vs. MFN tariff reduction. Each point represents a 4-digit Standard International Trade Classification (SITC) product (1,150 products). Change in MFN vs. change in preferential tariffs from 1994–2012.

Source: Data generated in Stata file, in all Mexican, Canadian, and US outliers (MFN increase above twenty-five) are dropped for variation to be visible (no bunching). For Mexico, seventeen outliers dropped (less than 2 percent of data).

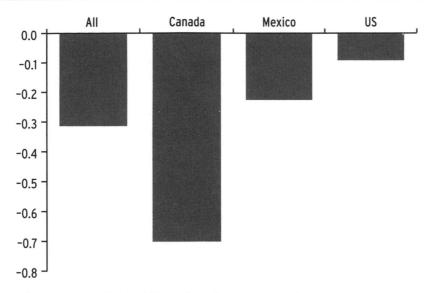

Figure 4.12 MFN tariffs and preference margins.
Source: Data generated in Stata file, in all Mexican, Canadian, and US outliers (MFN increase above twenty-five) are dropped for variation to be visible (no bunching). For Canada, one outlier dropped.

Boskin: The benefits could be as large as, or larger than, just the direct benefits, right?

Freund: Absolutely. As an overall evaluation, trade creation has dominated diversion. Preferences appear to have promoted external tariff reductions in all of the NAFTA countries.

One of the questions is, if NAFTA is so successful, why is there opposition? We have touched on some of these reasons. One is anti-globalization, which was maybe stronger in the past than it is now, as the supply chains and people have realized that you need to be in countries and companies that compete globally for success.

It has also been a period where unemployment around the world is high. Wages have stagnated. Outsourcing has become a touchy subject. There is a lot of inequality. This was, as mentioned earlier, the first comprehensive North-South deal. That opened up the issues of labor and the environment. There was also the proximity, the neighborhood effect, and concerns over migration and drugs. The US trade deficits, which have been so difficult to address over this whole period of NAFTA, are another.

Still, liberalization is moving forward, as we know. I hope that it will help to deepen NAFTA as well. TPP would increase NAFTA by about 75 percent in terms of both merchandise trade and population. Finally, what might the TPP add to NAFTA? This goes to the question of what was missing. Freer trade, but not completely free trade in agriculture. There are state-owned enterprises, coverage of government procurement, labor, the environment, expanded e-commerce, intellectual property rights, new approaches to rules of origin, potentially a currency chapter, and potentially cyber-espionage. What is also interesting are the issues that are not on the list, like migration and contingent protection.

Bagwell: Lorenzo, your welfare numbers for the US and Canada were small. That might be different from what some might have expected. Can you tell us a little bit more about what is behind those numbers?

Caliendo: As I showed you, real income has increased. That basically means real wages. Welfare implies whether we have an income to purchase things that we consume. These are estimates that reflect our purchasing power in terms of the goods that we can consume: does it go up or down? That is what I mean by welfare. It is not only income, income that comes from wages and also income that comes from tariff revenue. We have to adjust by the prices of the goods and the baskets of the goods that we consume.

First, the numbers are small in general. That is not something about this study, or NAFTA, but is a challenge for the international trade literature in general. We still need to understand what the real welfare gains are from trade. We are able to find large trade effects from tariff reductions. I can argue for large effects on real wages. When we go back to the welfare measures, most of the studies have found—and this is a challenge for international trade literature—that the welfare effects are small.

I think this is mainly because some channels are missing, i.e., the channels that Dan pointed out, gains in productivity and heterogeneity across firms. In terms of productivity, it might actually improve welfare gains in general, although there is some tension about this in the literature.

Most of the tariff reductions in my analysis came from the US to Mexico, Canada to Mexico, and vice versa. The tariffs between Canada and the US were really small back then. That is behind the results on welfare for Canada and the US. The smaller economy here is Mexico. In trade, the smaller economies are the ones that always gain the most, like Ukraine having the chance to open with a very large economy like Europe.

Jaime Serra Puche: I must say that I am very happy to see that the trade diversion in NAFTA is small. That is what I used to tell the newspaper people after every negotiation. People were saying that it was going to be very trade-diverting. When I left the government, I went to teach for a year in Princeton. I invited Carla and Michael, as well as some other people, to write a little book on trade diversion and regionalism. We wrote a little book called *Reflections on Regionalism,* published by the Carnegie Foundation.

When we answered that it was not going to be diversion, we were being politicians. We did not know if there was going to be diversion or not. When we studied it, it turns out that the role of the rules of origin is more relevant than the role of tariffs in the analysis of trade diversion.

I am raising this point because I think your work is fantastic, how you compare MFN to preferential tariffs. You should probably look into the issues of rules of origin. I think what could be derived from that analysis is that the rules of the GATT, or the WTO rules, are stronger because of the discipline you have to have in your MFN tariff than in your rules of origin.

A very important issue, if we believe in free trade agreements as building blocks for global trade, we need to change some of the rules in the WTO, especially Article XXIV,[7] because they do not have a

---

7. Article XXIV: Territorial Application–Frontier Traffic–Customs Unions and Free-trade Areas, http://www.wto.org/english/res_e/booksp_e/analytic_index_e /gatt1994_09_e.htm on formation of preferential agreements despite MFN rules.

condition of maximum component of rules of origin. This came from Jacob Viner's book[8] on the cost of customs unions. Back then, when the GATT created these rules, there were very few FTAs. Most of them were customs unions. Now it is the other way around; customs unions are very few, and now we have FTAs that have rules of origin.

Introducing rules in order to discipline the rules of origin is crucial. In the case of NAFTA, we found that we did not introduce too much of a distortion because of the history of our trade. The content that we ended up negotiating with Carla and Michael for rules of origin was pretty much the reflection of our history. We were pretty integrated in that sense. I think you can conclude nicely that we did not create trade diversion, not only through tariff reduction or through the differentiation between MFN and preferential tariffs, but also because of the rules of origin.

That does not mean the rules of origin should not be regulated. I believe that in the WTO they should regulate rules of origin.

Daniel Trefler: I will try to integrate four very disparate mechanisms for thinking about trade and to make sure we understand which are complementary and which are overlapping.

The core of what Lorenzo is getting at, which no one has been able to do before, are these inter-industry linkages that allow us to talk about things like supply chains. That is hugely important and completely novel. In fact, I told a PhD student, before I had read his paper, that what he was doing could not be done. The key that is novel here in terms of policymaking is that we are getting at the internal linkages, which we have never been able to do before. The numbers that we are seeing relate to those inter-industry linkages. That is one piece of the gains.

Then we have Caroline's discussion of another piece, the trade diversion and creation, which adds additional numbers to our welfare-gain

---

8. Jacob Viner, *The Customs Union Issue* (Washington, DC: Carnegie Endowment for International Peace, 1950).

calculations. We are getting more gains from that, although Caroline put it in trade terms rather than in welfare terms.

We had Stephen's discussion of an equally important gain, which is what the impacts of these agreements are on the way we function as a society. He talked about democratization of Mexico, which is a whole other set of gains. Who knows how large those are? Yet, they are fundamental to the way we want to think about the gains from trade.

Democratization is one source of gains, but with democratization also comes something that George is interested in. That is an increase in the provision of public goods, like K–12 education in Mexico. They are under-provided precisely because of the monopoly of power in Mexico that NAFTA is helping to break.

What I am doing in my work is identifying yet another source of gains. I add on to the gains identified by Lorenzo, Caroline, and Stephen rather than overlap with them. The source I focus on starts with the fact that the vast majority of what we trade in manufactured goods and services is dominated by a very small number of mega-firms, the Walmarts of the world, the General Motors of the world, the Apples of the world. In my work we see that these firms adopt new technologies strategically. They think about how they are going to position themselves in a market. Can they create value in that market? They adopt active strategies to make sure that value is created. The resulting NAFTA-induced innovation adds further welfare gains into the pot.

To be more concrete, in the case of Mexico, what the US market offered for Mexican firms was not that they could continue making Volkswagen Beetles in crummy factories that had no robotics and no quality control and no skilled labor. What NAFTA gave Mexican firms was demanding American consumers who were not going to accept any of those autos. What mattered was the type of market the US offered to these firms. It was the demanding US consumers that forced the Mexican firms to say they could not keep producing lousy Volkswagen VWs and must produce something entirely different. It is not about trade diversion. It is all about trade creation. You wonderful NAFTA negotiators gave the opportunity, and now strategically the firms have taken advantage of that.

So what I am saying is that the gains from NAFTA identified by Lorenzo, Caroline, Stephen, and myself are distinct, and it is the sum total of these gains that is the legacy of NAFTA.

Serra Puche: I am the son of refugees. My parents came from Spain. They came from a civil war. We were always a very close family without much money. I used to be a bit jealous in school when a kid would wear a T-shirt that his father brought from the US. I could not afford that; my parents did not fly to the US and buy clothes.

In Mexico, we used to use the following term: export quality. When you think about that term, it is grotesque. We are saying that we are going to produce better for the foreigners, not for our own consumers. That is what happens when you close your economy and you protect it. Producers take advantage of the fact that the country is protected. You produce crummy Beetles but a very nice Jetta for American drivers or for Canadian drivers. That was common in Mexico. Mexicans are thinking that they should produce better products for people abroad than domestically. That is a pretty wild idea when you think about it.

But this has changed in Mexico, dramatically. You are right. Our exports are not crummy. We produce some Beetles in a wonderful plant in Puebla. Now we produce almost all the cars that are consumed in the US.

Boskin: I would add to this as a side interest of mine. Almost certainly, your price indexes do not account enough for the quality improvement of the goods. The real wage gains may be even larger. That is a big problem, even in our price indexes.

Basic trade theory suggests that bilateral trade should be a function of the product of the size of the economies and a decreasing function of the distance between them as a proxy for transportation costs. Hence the name "gravity model," like Newton's law of gravity.

An undergraduate honors student of mine, Ed Zhu, estimated these and looked at all the trade agreements. He was very interested in trying to figure out what a Japan/China/Korea free trade agreement might be able to do. He estimated them by looking at a gravity model, estimated not only for the whole period but at different sub-periods, before and after the FTAs. He concluded that NAFTA, conditional on GDP growth and all these changes Lorenzo mentioned, increased trade by 84 percent. The effect of NAFTA was the largest of any of the trade agreements.

Getting at the diversion issue raised by Caroline and Kyle is the more recent trade theory. There has been a renaissance in trade theory, which is great from my perspective as an intellectual historian. You guys have developed models that enable some notion of the orderings of comparative advantage. It seems to me that you could look into the details of that, even beyond what Caroline has done, to see where the next-lowest cost producers might have been and look at diversion there. Maybe that is a needle in a haystack. Is that doable, Kyle, do you think?

Bagwell: I think we have the people in the room here, empirical people, who could do that. They are all nodding their heads. I take reassurance in that.

Trefler: Not only for which country, but actually which products.

Boskin: It seems to me that this may be the next frontier of the academic research in this area that can profitably be pursued.

Michael H. Wilson: While the analyses that we have been talking about are important to understand, as well as some of these outcomes, it is most important to me to go back to why Mexico went into the NAFTA negotiations. You were not considering trade diversion. You had some basic goals related to the structure of the Mexican economy and the transformation that you wanted under Salinas's government, though the effects of NAFTA started to move the economy and the structure of the country away from them.

Our goals were different from Mexico's, but we too had broad goals that we wanted to achieve by moving into a closer relationship with the United States and, subsequently, into the NAFTA with Mexico. I think we have to judge the success of NAFTA against how it produced positive results against our two sets of criteria for going into the deals.

Yes, the various ingredients to support that are important. But we cannot lose sight of those broader reasons and the great success that we both achieved. The United States probably did not gain to the same extent, but the fact that you have two much healthier countries to your north and south is a very important part of the benefits that the United States achieved on this. I think that is the message.

Diego Perez: Lorenzo, you showed us that the links between the US and Mexico were high, as well as the links between the US and Canada. The trade links between Mexico and Canada were not so high. My question is whether you have a rough idea of how much of your quantified welfare gains could have been attained if, as opposed to signing NAFTA, there had been two FTAs signed, one between the US and Mexico and the other one between the US and Canada.

Caliendo: That is a great question. We have not done that particular exercise, but what we have is the following. As I mentioned, many agreements were signed during this period. Using this methodology, we can fit the real numbers into this model and ask if, by the year 2005 when many agreements actually happened, all except NAFTA, to what extent NAFTA helped Mexico, Canada, and the US to gain, given that they were also signing those other agreements? We find that the welfare measures are actually larger than what I showed you. That is answering another question. NAFTA potentially could have helped indirectly benefit other agreements. We have not done that particular exercise, which is very important.

We need a unifying way to measure the objective functions of the governments that are negotiating, in terms of that measure of the gains. That is a unifying framework that we should be after as academics. I guess all incentives are aligned, and that is where we are going.

Serra Puche: What is better, three bilaterals or one trilateral? The reason I was asking myself this question is because a few years ago, Michael, your colleagues in Canada were pushing for more of a bilateral progress with the US, rather than injecting that energy into the trilateral commitment.

I think there are more issues here than you could probably simulate in Lorenzo's model. First, there is the scale of the market, which is not irrelevant. Second, there are logistics, innovation, and exchange, which are also not irrelevant. If we take the step of moving on the labor front and letting the community develop, as George was saying, allowing a region to have free mobility of capital, labor, and merchandise, will add some welfare gains that are bigger than three bilateral agreements. It would be an interesting exercise. I assume your model can accommodate that.

Mary O'Grady: If we agree that more free trade is good and we agree that more access to inputs for producing is good, then if we look at something like the Pacific Alliance,[9] would it be in the interests of NAFTA members to say they want to change the rules of origin to include producers in the Pacific Alliance? If NAFTA did that, would that clearly be trade diversion? I have been thinking a lot about how you make the trade area bigger and bigger.

Since the WTO does not seem to be working very well, I think that the Pacific Alliance is a creative way to expand trade in Latin American countries that are trying to liberalize more, as opposed to those that are more closed. Does something like that make sense for the expansion of trade in the region, or is it too much? Would it cause too much diversion?

Freund: I want to couple that with the point made earlier about rules of origin. They are really a thorn in the side of all of this liberalization. In our study, the creation numbers should still come through, because to the extent that a margin is bigger, the rules of origin would be bigger, which would then come through in the estimates on the trade flows. I do not think it would affect our estimates. It probably

---

9. Members are Chile, Colombia, Mexico, and Peru, with Costa Rica in the process of joining in 2014.

reduces it. I do not know what the creation or diversion would be in the absence of the rules of origin. These are the ones with existing rules of origin.

I guess economists often deal with rules of origin, as the group gets bigger, by accumulating them. That means that within the group, the local content has to come from the group. That is the discussion, for example, in the potential TPP. It seems that as long as you accumulate them, you are going to improve upon the existing situation. The ideal way would be to discipline them in the WTO and have a standard that they can only be a certain percentage. Cumulation, with the rules of origin, means that with 25 percent local content, it can come from this country or from another country in the agreement.

O'Grady: Does that mean that you could add? Say you wanted to add Peru. You want to change the rules of origin for NAFTA for things that are coming from the Pacific Alliance. Would it be in the interest of the NAFTA countries to do something like that? Would that be very diversionary?

Serra Puche: I think that, within the Alliance, most of those countries already have free trade agreements with everybody. It means that every single agreement they have has a rule of origin. The rule of origin applies to the specific agreement. If I want to export this microphone, the steel has to come from North America: from Canada, from the US, or from Mexico. If we add Peru, the steel could come from Peru. That is accumulation of the rules of origin.

I think US policymakers need to decide whether they want to open up that possibility. George was saying that for every dollar we export, 40 cents are American inputs, intermediate inputs. For the Peruvians, this is much lower. From the rest of the Pacific Alliance or for the TPP, it is much lower. So the consequences for American industry or the American economy are not minor.

For countries that want to export to the US market, for example, Mexico, it would be fine to have the possibility to get inputs from Peru, if we find that a very competitive input.

Freund: It would be opening up the possibility. My instinct is that it would have to be creationary. It is hard to see where a diversionary effect would come.

Serra Puche: You might be right. I just have not thought that through.

Alan Sykes: Related to this rules-of-origin discussion, one bit of lore among trade law practitioners is that a lot of NAFTA trade that could qualify for NAFTA preferences does not claim it because the transaction costs of claiming and proving compliance with the rules of origin exceed the value of the preference. I am just curious if anyone here has tried to get an empirical handle on what the magnitude of that problem is. The related question is how much money is spent on the stuff that does get NAFTA treatment, proving compliance with NAFTA rules of origin.

Freund: There was a recent study done by some economists at the Graduate Institute (of International and Development Studies) in Geneva. They have overturned that result. The old thinking was that you needed a margin of 3 percent for eligible trade to take advantage of preferences. In looking at data at a very fine level, at the eight- and ten-digit levels instead of the six-digit level, they found that almost all margins are actually being taken advantage of. It is really a very small percentage of trade that is eligible for preferences and not taking advantage of preference margins.

Serra Puche: We built, during the negotiations of rules of origin, a general equilibrium model for NAFTA. We simulated different rules of origin. We kept on comparing the rules of origin we negotiated with Carla and Michael, focusing on the effect that would have on the supply chain in Mexico. Most of the cases did not have a big change. We did not find big distortions. I think that 90 percent-plus of Mexican exports that are going into the US comply with rules of origin.

The methodology that is chosen to check that this has happened is on a case-by-case demand. People in Mexico say, "These people from Illinois are exporting this product to us and it does not fulfill the rules of origin." They go in and they analyze it. The number of cases has been quite small, given the size of trade. Still, rules of origin are a pain, I agree.

Hills: You also have to take into account that it affects small and medium-sized businesses disproportionately. When you say 80 percent or 90 percent of trade, that is an accurate statement. It is also accurate to say many small and medium-sized businesses no longer take advantage of NAFTA because of the onerous cost and time involved in meeting those requirements. Because in the United States small and medium-sized enterprises are the job creators, creating roughly 60 percent of our jobs, you really pinch the foot that is running in the race.

Chapter Five

North American Energy

The NAFTA nations are in a period of major change on the energy front, involving the fracking revolution, political and environmental debates, the possible opening of the Mexican petroleum industry to foreign investment, and greater export opportunities. James Sweeney, a professor of management science and engineering at Stanford, and Michael H. Wilson, former Canadian finance and international trade minister, bring their perspectives to the continent's future energy independence.

Presenters: James L. Sweeney, Michael H. Wilson

Comments: Thomas F. Stephenson, George P. Shultz, Jaime Serra Puche, Mary O'Grady, Michael J. Boskin, Stephen Haber, Daniel Trefler

Thomas Stephenson: As George Shultz mentioned, North America has emerged as a true entity and marketplace. I think about energy through the lens of a three-legged stool: national security, economic security, and environmental security. It has been an eventful twenty years for energy within North America, particularly in the last five or six years, with the huge impact of new approaches to exploring for unconventional oil and gas, the so-called fracking revolution.

First, its impact on national security: there is no question that North America is rapidly moving toward relative energy independence. We do not spend a lot of time worrying about OPEC[1] today, certainly not to the extent that we used to.

---

1. OPEC, the Organization of the Petroleum Exporting Countries, proclaimed an oil embargo on the US in 1973, which led to rationing and steeply higher prices.

Second, from an economic security standpoint, this energy revolution has had a very positive impact on the North American trade balance. There is a lot less money flowing to other parts of the world, and North America is beginning to export more natural resources.

Third, from an environmental security perspective, the substitution of natural gas for coal is having a very positive impact on CO_2 (carbon dioxide) emissions throughout North America. This unconventional oil and gas is being developed in the United States and Canada, very little in Mexico, more flowing to Mexico. But when you look at North America as a whole, the fracking revolution is having a dynamic impact on these three key elements.

From a trade facilitation and trade barrier standpoint, probably the two key issues are the Keystone XL pipeline and the changes in Mexico's approach to energy. The limitations on investment in Mexican energy today are a constraint on full development of resources. How is that going to shake out? If there is nothing more than profit-sharing, it will not have a big impact; you have to get production into the equation. The revenue implications are non-trivial for Mexico.

James Sweeney: I want to go back to the NAFTA text. Article I: eliminate barriers, promote competition. It did not say get rid of all problems. It said facilitate and strengthen. Chapter 6, on principles, recognizes it is desirable to strengthen the important role of trade in energy and petrochemicals. But, for Mexico, there was another provision: the parties confirm the full respect for their constitutions, and NAFTA does not include all energy. Canada does include all energy, which has led to some very positive consequences for Canada and maybe some negative consequences for Mexico.

When we deal with energy, rules of origin are really easy. If the oil is coming from Canada, it has been produced in Canada, no confusion about it. So, I like to use a simple, idealized version of a well-functioning NAFTA, and I will keep coming back to it, even though it is not the actual language. It says that the decisions between the three nations should be made as if there were no national boundaries between the producers and consumers. That is my idealized vision; forget that there are national boundaries. That does not mean only commercial considerations, because we pay attention to other things than just the commercial.

Consider the energy policy triangle, which is a trade-off among economic, environmental, and security issues. NAFTA should still take all of them into account as if there were no national boundaries. For energy trade between Canada and the US, that high ideal is operating with one sore thumb, the Keystone XL pipeline.

Between Mexico and the US, trade in commodities seems consistent, but Mexican regulatory issues have been limiting investment flows and may limit their own economic capabilities. Mexico has been left behind in the North American energy revolution, partly because the Mexicans have not made changes in their constitution; but it is their constitution, not ours.

The one issue in which we are not operating as if there were no national boundaries is in the Keystone XL pipeline.

Examine the data in figure 5.1 on natural gas trade. US natural gas imports peaked around the year 2000. From 2004 through 2006 the number flattened and has since been declining. Basically, most of the natural gas that the United States imports is from Canada. We do import liquefied natural gas, LNG, and we are now a net exporter of natural gas to Mexico. Mexico has tremendous natural gas reserves, but now the US has become the net exporter in natural gas. The US also exports natural gas to Canada. For natural gas, North America is basically self-sufficient when you add the three together.

To ask if there are trade barriers, compare the prices going in opposite directions, and you notice that, between Canada and the US, prices move the same. Natural gas prices vary from $2 up to $12 per thousand cubic feet. The market has been working exactly the way you want a natural resource market to work. Prices go up and down with market conditions. A very healthy market is happening in natural gas. The trade value of natural gas between Canada and the US has plummeted, simply because the price of natural gas has gone down with normal market forces. The quantities that we in the United States import from Canada are going down. US imports are down to half a billion dollars per month from $4 billion a month; the trade balances have been moving around sharply

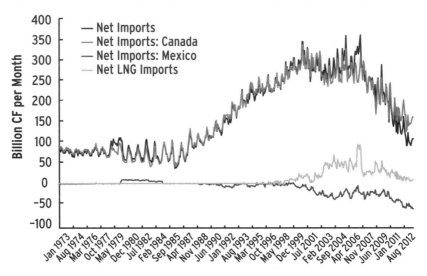

Figure 5.1 North American natural gas trade (monthly).
Source: Data from "US Natural Gas Imports by Country," US Energy Information Administration, http://www.eia.gov/dnav/ng/ng_move_impc_s1_m.htm.

between Canada and the US. Between Mexico and the US, it is a very small number.

What has happened is the shale revolution. The US is now producing a lot of natural gas from shale. In estimates of how much is available of technically recoverable shale gas resources the US is the largest of the three, but Mexico is not far behind. The geologists are saying Mexico may have a lot of potential for producing natural gas from shale.

Electricity: the US imports significant electricity from Canada (see figure 5.2). We export to Canada and we trade with Mexico. Canada and the US have become very aggressive trading partners. The quantities of electricity are going up and down in a very robust way, varying by the hourly, daily, and weekly changes in market conditions, a sign of an extremely healthy electricity market.

Because electricity cannot be stored, there are times when it has a very high value south of the Canadian border. Other times it has a particularly high value north of the border. So, you can envision a lot of trade flow. Canada is dominantly a hydropower system. It can store water in a reservoir and it is just like a very big battery, because you can choose when to store it. The US is mostly a thermal system and

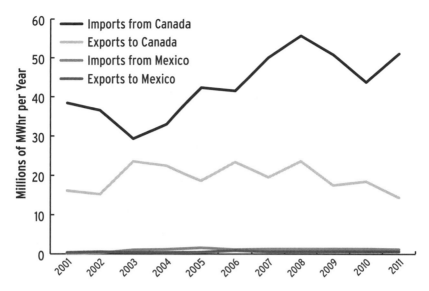

Figure 5.2 US electricity trade.

Source: Data from National Energy Board of Canada and US Department of Energy. US Department of Energy, Office of Electricity Delivery & Energy Reliability, Form OE-781R, "Report of International Electricity Import/Export Data," predecessor forms. To estimate electricity trade with Mexico for 2001, forward data from the California Independent System Operator are used in combination with the Form OE-781R values.

you cannot store it. So you have lots of opportunity for the equivalent of arbitrage between the two. There may be very little net flow and a very high value. British Columbia is roughly on balance with the US over time, yet there is very high value for both sides because the hydro system of British Columbia is complementary to the thermal system of the United States, with large potential gains.

The North American coal trade works in the other direction. The US exports small quantities of coal to Canada. It imports a little bit from Canada and Mexico. The increase of US coal exports is mostly to the European countries, as we are moving away from coal, which releases relatively large amounts of carbon dioxide. We are exporting it to the European countries, including the Netherlands, who now are burning that coal.

For petroleum, the exports from Canada to the United States continue to grow at a quite rapid rate. Canada and Mexico used to be about the same; now Mexico is about one sixth as large in gross

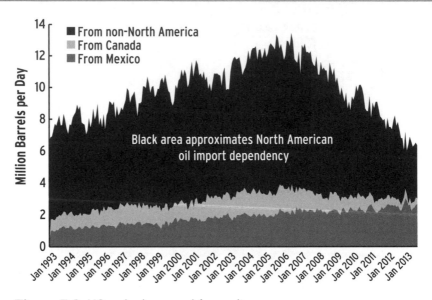

Figure 5.3 US petroleum net imports.

Source: Data from "US Net Imports by Country," US Energy Information Administration, http://www.eia.gov/dnav/pet/pet_move_neti_a_ep00_imn_mbblpd_m.htm.

exports to the United States. But Mexico imports crude oil, and production is almost equal to the amount of exports.

Figure 5.3 shows that we are rapidly moving to a situation of North American oil self-sufficiency. North America is moving toward self-sufficiency, depending upon fuel efficiency standards for automobiles and on the Keystone XL pipeline.

Figure 5.4 looks at the total trade values of net energy exports: from Canada to the United States, $80 billion is oil. The rest is quantitatively small but strategically large, particularly the electricity, because failure to have electricity when you need it leads to blackouts. In the 2000–2001 Western electricity crisis, electricity exports from British Columbia made all the difference between California having only a small—rather than a large—number of blackouts.

Energy trade is robust between Canada and the United States; but between Mexico and the United States, their own internal issues are limiting development of their resources.

The Keystone XL pipeline is a pipeline system that is bringing oil, both from Canada to the Gulf Coast, and from northern parts of the

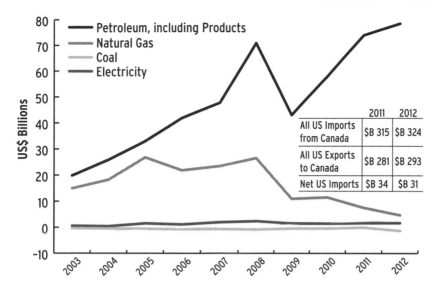

Figure 5.4 Value of energy net exports: Canada to US.

Source: Data from "US Imports from Canada by 5-digit End-Use Code 2004–2013," US Census Bureau, http://www.census.gov/foreign-trade/statistics/product/enduse/imports/c1220.html.

United States to our Gulf Coast. Parts are already constructed. That is not the controversy. The controversy is the part that would bring in oil across the border from Canada to the United States, about 830,000 barrels per day. If you multiply that by a $100 price, that is $25 billion a year. This is not an insignificant issue. But, as opposed to other US-Canadian energy, where there is normal trade going on, construction of the pipeline segment requires presidential approval.

The proponents—and I am one—see national security and economic benefits of the Keystone XL pipeline. The better trade we have in oil, the better national security we have, and the economic benefits are quite real. The opponents see greenhouse gas emissions from the oil sands and assert other environmental risks of moving oil by pipeline, even though all of the evidence is that the safest way of moving oil is by pipeline, much safer than by train. So, the question is, what if we did not have the pipeline, what would be the consequence? My belief is that Canada will produce just about as much oil, but either ship it by rail, some to the United States, at a cost of $6 to $10 a barrel more and with more environmental damage and more risk, or Canada can expand some pipelines that go west and ship it to China, and we would lose national security benefits.

We gain nothing for the environment by blocking pipeline construction, but the pipeline to bring oil from Canadian oil sands to market in the United States has become a massive symbolic issue. If you are worried about global climate change—and I am—you might compare the carbon dioxide emissions per unit of energy in Canadian oil to that of the coal we export to Canada. You would see that we are exporting a more carbon dioxide–intense commodity than the one that opponents of the Keystone XL pipeline find unacceptable to import from Canada. And Venezuela's heavy oil is similar in carbon dioxide emissions to the oil from the Canadian oil sands, which has about 10–15 percent more than the average US oil. So we are not talking about massive differences, but 10–15 percent, which figures right within the area of variability of other oil that we import.

The decision is being held up by what appear to me basically presidential and congressional political considerations, not environmental or security or energy issues.

George P. Shultz: What is happening, Jim, is that the president is performing what might be called a pocket veto, not taking any action. He does not want to face up to it. And the result of that is that the company involved is about to cancel the pipeline and go other ways, so I have been told. But this is a tragedy. When I was secretary of labor, I was given the job by the president to study the oil import program in 1969. We could easily see that there was instability in the Middle East due to Arab-Israeli tensions and we made a number of recommendations of what to do about it. None were accepted. So I am secretary of the Treasury in 1973 and along comes exactly what we said to watch out for. Now, anybody who thinks the Middle East is a region of great stability right now must be living somewhere else. So here we have oil that does not go through the Strait of Hormuz. It is an absolute no-brainer, but it is just drifting, and the president will be able to kill it by just not doing anything, which is characteristic.

Sweeney: I believe it is time we move forward with the pipeline approval and eliminate the very sore and deep issue that is moving us away from an idealized vision of NAFTA: that the decisions on energy trade between the three nations should be made as if there were no national boundaries between them.

Michael H. Wilson: Up until now, the energy trade flows between the United States and Canada, for as long as we have had oil, which goes back to 1957, and for all the energy that we export by means of natural gas and electricity, have been very smooth. We have one issue that stands in the way. In fact, that is *the* main issue between the United States and Canada. Thanks to NAFTA and the dispute settlement agreement, the trade flows between the countries are remarkably quiet; even softwood lumber has gone quiet, although that bubbles up periodically. But that is why Keystone has gotten such a high profile: because it is unusual.

Between now and 2030, we are going to have two million barrels a day more of oil; this creates a real problem if we continue to have this attitude toward increased flows. In figure 5.5, you can see that the gaps in exports are quite significant; that is a market-based issue that we have to deal with. That has nothing to do with any regulations. It has everything to do with the shale gas revolution.

And figure 5.6 shows how the amount of shale gas in the United States is swamping what we are selling into the United States. The Alberta Clipper (pipeline) issue was approved in September of 2009 with the same considerations of national security of supply and environmental issues. The State Department had a good analysis of the importance of both, and came down with a pretty balanced set of views that the Alberta Clipper oil pipeline should go ahead. It is not a large pipeline, largely from the oil sands as well, with the same considerations.

The Keystone XL inaction is very troublesome. It is a pocket veto. It is very frustrating, because we have good supporters in the United States. But the environmental opponents of this are very vociferous, have gained a lot of attention, and will continue to gain attention as the delay continues. I would say it is quite ironic. Remember that Jim

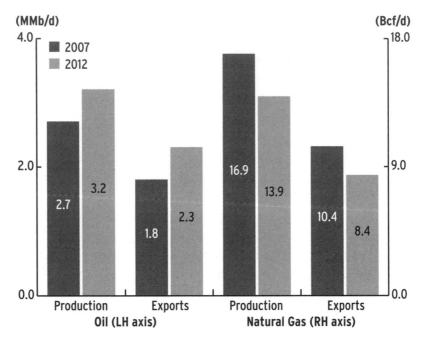

Figure 5.5 Canadian market evolution.
Source: Data from "Energy Statistics Handbook," Statistics Canada; Canadian Association of Petroleum Producers "Crude Oil Forecast, Markets & Transportation."

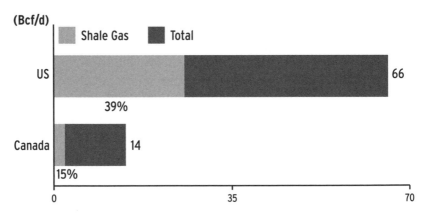

Figure 5.6 US shale gas revolution.
Source: "North America leads the world in production of shale gas," US Energy Information Administration, http://www.eia.gov/todayinenergy/detail.cfm?id=13491.

Sweeney showed the coal exports just skyrocketing. Well, that is causing some real problems in Europe, where some major recipients of this
coal are not able to meet their environmental targets. It is the cheap
coal from the United States that the electric companies are buying,
and have to buy, because it makes business sense for them.

But it is the combination of the Keystone issue, which is a politically motivated position, and the market issue of shale gas which has
presented Canada with a watershed decision. Because all of our oil
and natural gas have gone to one market, the United States, we are
being forced now for market reasons—and also for political reasons—
to consider alternatives. The resource is too important. The size of
energy flows that we have, and the two million barrels a day that are
on target to be available, are something we cannot ignore. And the
result is that we are going to have to look elsewhere to sell that energy.

What options do we have on the oil side? We have two million
barrels a day coming onstream. We have the third largest oil reserves
in the world; 97 percent of these are in oil sands. If we cannot sell it
to the United States, we have to look to Asia, to Europe. It will certainly result in a diversion of the balance between the United States
and these other countries and likely result in lower volumes going to
the United States. If we do not get the increased Keystone capacity,
we are going to be forced to do this, because we just cannot leave it
in the ground.

Natural gas is a market-based issue that we have to deal with. We
are looking at LNG exports or exports through upgrading into petrochemicals or urea, for example. There are several LNG terminals that
are being proposed for our West Coast. There is a significant infrastructure challenge there, but we simply must make these decisions
because we need time to get that infrastructure in place.

I believe this North American integration will continue. You need
the energy. We have thirty natural gas pipelines between the two
countries and twenty oil pipelines. The existing capacity is 3.6 million barrels a day, and the 3.2 million barrels per day of production
certainly can be handled by the pipeline we have. But, as these new
projects come onstream, that is going to quickly increase. What we
are looking at is three million barrels a day of proposed capacity. It

is a significant amount, but where do we put it? Can we do anything north-south, or do we have to go east or west?

For every two oil-sands jobs created in Canada, there is one that will be created in the United States. So, there is an economic reason. Our estimate is 440,000 incremental US jobs by 2035.

Offshore will provide us with flexibility and, quite frankly, flexibility in future bargaining. One existing pipeline comes down through North Dakota, which soon will be your number two oil-producing state after Texas. The trans-Canada pipeline going through that state takes a lot of Bakken[2] oil down to Oklahoma and the Gulf Coast refineries. I jokingly say to myself, "Well, why don't we just ship all Canadian oil through that pipeline and demonstrate that we are important to the broader energy interests of the United States?"

We therefore have a major infrastructure challenge. We have environmentalists in Canada who are going to make sure that everything is taken into account. The government has put in place a system whereby all of the approvals will be the subject of one hearing, so that the different interested regulators will be involved in one hearing in order to speed up the process.

One of our most important national issues is that the First Nations have put the country on notice that they are not going to let any of these pipelines that go to the West Coast, LNG terminals or pipelines for British Columbia, unless they get some treaty claims approved that have been outstanding for a long time. That is probably going to be a bigger challenge to us than the environmental issue. They have been making some very strong statements recently and there are certainly grounds for them to take the positions that they have. Not all First Nations are the same; some are more willing to be commercially oriented. But there will be some along the routes that will be much more hawkish.

Let me go back to looking at this as a North American region. There are a number of benefits if we become a self-sufficient global energy leader in natural gas and oil. We are there in natural gas, as Jim

---

2. The Bakken formation underlies parts of Montana, North Dakota, Saskatchewan, and Manitoba.

Sweeney's charts have shown. Collectively, the three countries can, by 2020, be fully self-sufficient in oil. We have cost advantages, but we also have availability advantages that I think will accrue to our benefit. On the environmental side, I think that this can be done with a positive North American impact. As I said, we have put in a new project review process. Some in the United States are saying that is something that the United States should adopt.

Constitutional reform in Mexico is a key component to this whole picture. But it is important to have an open trilateral dialogue so that we understand the issues each country is dealing with and can take them into account, not as a single decision-making process, but as a guide to what we can do to develop the resources and meet the needs of the North American economy in the most effective way, and at a minimum avoid energy policies or regulations that upset the normal flows.

The shale energy revolution, which is turning the whole industry on its ear, is underway and shows signs of continuing for quite a while. We have to resolve the Keystone XL challenge, which is more than just one pipeline: it is a signal for future pipelines. And then we must resolve what is happening in Mexico.

My conclusion is that we need an energy dialogue, the capacity to exchange views on what is happening, taking into account the different perspectives of the three countries. This will require an ongoing, high-level dialogue. The leadership on this one is absolutely critical, and the three countries have got to agree at a very senior level to do it, if it is going to be effective.

Jaime Serra Puche: As we speak, the Mexican Senate is debating a constitutional change that is different from the original proposal the government sent. The original proposal the government sent was to change literally two words in the Constitution in an article in which both licenses and production-sharing are forbidden. The idea was just to leave the one that forbids licenses. Apparently, after the debate with the PAN, they sent a more aggressive proposal, which is to allow everything, including licenses, production-sharing, profit-sharing and so on. And they are going to do it. A full opening of energy would

put certain procedures into the Constitution. So, in a very unortho-
dox way, they are changing certain elements, that ideally belonged in
implementing the legislation, directly into the Constitution instead.

For a constitutional change, you need two-thirds of the Senate and
two-thirds of the House. The PRI and PAN have it. And then you
need a simple majority with the state legislatures, which the PAN and
the PRI also have. So, it is not a matter of votes. It is quite possible it will happen. The leader of the PRD, the left, Andrés Manuel
López Obrador, had a heart attack a week ago, and given the politics
in Mexico, some people are saying that it was an induced heart attack
so that he could not fight against this measure. But even if it is not
orthodox to make all those changes in the Constitution, it might be
the only way to do it right now, which eventually will reflect in the
implementing legislation.

How quickly will the market react to this? I have talked to some
large companies in the US and they say that they have two significant
conditions before they start moving projects. The first is the ability
for companies that invest in Mexico, under this new regime, to book
reserves. Reserve booking is absolutely essential to them, because otherwise the value of their shares can be affected.

Mary O'Grady: That is in the transitory articles.

Serra Puche: The reason for that transitory article is that the government is claiming that the reserves still belong to the state. The
companies are already talking to the SEC (Securities and Exchange
Commission) to see what they need, even if you have the ideologi-
cal principle that the reserves belong to the state. That is challenge
number one.

Second, they do not want to deal with the oil union; they do not
want to get involved with those guys. They are right; it is a very corrupt and complicated union. Companies are going to have to put pressure on the Labor Department in Mexico so that private investors
in energy have their own union, not one union for the whole sector,
which is what the current union wants to do. It is a big issue, but I
think it will be resolved. Today there is only one union that works

for the whole industry. It wants to keep that power, though the private investors want them to open up. This is a politically complicated issue.

O'Grady: It is my impression that the union pension fund liabilities are unfunded. Is that a negotiating point for the government? Peña Nieto might say to the union, "You know, you don't have any money." And then they might be willing to trade some concessions.

Serra Puche: Having put the boss of the teachers' union into jail is a much stronger sign than the pension funds.

O'Grady: Salinas did that, too, didn't he?

Serra Puche: My recommendation is that we not do it through NAFTA. Actually, probably the most complicated provision says that you have some guarantee of supply. That is, for instance, if Canada lowers production by one million barrels, the Canadians keep on exporting the same proportion to the US.

An annex to Article 625 says this condition applies to all the parties, but not to Mexico. Mexico did not go for the guarantee, thinking that we were the surplus country. With the new projections, it is not clear that we will be the surplus country, so we were probably shooting ourselves in the foot with that exception. But linking the current energy reform in Mexico with the NAFTA proposal would not help reform in Mexico, but hurt it. Mexico is going to need a year or so after this change to start bringing the issue to the North American formula. It will happen, but Mexico will have to manage it with great care, because things will be complicated politically after it is approved.

Stephenson: One of the things you have talked about previously was how the Mexican government will make up for the revenue stream from oil and gas today if some of this cash flow is diverted into revenues and profits for those developing the resources in the US and elsewhere.

Serra Puche: Mexico depends on oil revenue for public finance. One third of the revenue the government earns comes from energy. The government introduced an aggressive tax reform a few weeks ago to raise revenues from indirect taxation and corporate income tax, to compensate for the taxes they are going to sacrifice with the opening of Pemex.[3] Hopefully, they will be able to manage that issue over time.

Wilson: The oil and gas in Canada is owned by the provinces; they own the resource, i.e., Alberta owns the oil sands. So if Imperial or Exxon comes in, it gets the right to explore and produce the oil on a certain property. The ownership is still with the province.

Serra Puche: But can they book the value of the reserves on their balance sheet?

Wilson: Yes.

Michael Boskin: Yes; I do not know whether it is interactive with the production-sharing agreement, but definitely Exxon is booking reserves from Kearl,[4] for example.

Serra Puche: That is the condition that the main producers have, and I think it makes sense. In Mexico, the concept of owning your reserves is a bit more complicated than it is in Canada. People see it as their own property.

The shale gas will be open, no matter what shape the reform takes, because everybody realizes that it is essential. Electricity is going to be fully open, which I think is very good news.

Boskin: The SEC comment letter most commonly received by energy companies is about reserve bookings. A few years ago, Shell,

---

3. Petróleos Mexicanos, the Mexican oil monopoly.
4. The Kearl Oil Sands Project in Alberta.

which is generally regarded as a pretty well-run company, had a big scandal about this which cost the CEO his job. It is a very sensitive issue.

Serra Puche: What is the SEC inquiring?

Boskin: The questions generally are about the criteria you are using. You find the oil; discover a prospect; estimate first what is there, then what is economically, commercially recoverable from it, under what terms and what time period, etc. The SEC is very interested in the corporation's oversight of the individual engineering team and what it is doing. It is a big deal. There is a disclosure issue, and the SEC demands certain ways to calculate it so it is consistent across firms. And it is therefore requiring some well-run companies to state a number that the companies think is improper.

The shale revolution, oil sands, and the prospect of Mexico's opening up to foreign investment constitute one of the great geopolitical shifts in our favor in my lifetime. It will greatly reduce the strategic power of OPEC. It is immensely important. We could get more value out of that on the natural gas side if we were permitting export terminals and creating more of a global market. Natural gas costs $9 to $12 (per thousand cubic feet) in Europe, $15-plus in Japan, but just $4 here. And it is very hard to get an export terminal approved.

Before the shale revolution, companies were trying to permit import terminals. Now they are trying to permit export terminals. But if you want to do something that really helps global stability, figure out a way to get more natural gas to Europe from somewhere besides Russia, for example. I think that is another no-brainer.

It is also important to appreciate that there are large natural field declines. So to produce the same amount of oil or natural gas ten years from now as we are producing today will require us to find and produce, and hence to invest, an immense amount just to stay even. So it is important to understand that the target is moving. We are getting less and less from Alaska and the North Sea, for example.

We have complicated issues with the environment, which we have the opportunity to deal with in the medium term using natural gas to sub out coal. But it will be a while before we can get alternatives that scale to significance environmentally or economically. The energy industry is vast; it is almost unimaginable how much energy is produced and consumed. We are talking about billions of barrels of oil, trillions of cubic feet of gas, and trillions of dollars in necessary exploration and production investment. Thus, it will be some time before we have alternatives that are available on a scale without massive government subsidies to distort incentives, so that we can rely less on oil, for example. You can have an aggressive but economically, scientifically, and numerically literate policy, but the notion that you can shut off oil right now, for example, or oil sands production, does not pass a common-sense test.

We have to manage the policy so that we have a sensible set of economic and environmental outcomes over time.

Shultz: Your comments about the geopolitical significance of these developments are right on the mark. But I think it goes further, because if there are accompanying declines in price, then Saudi Arabia, which basically exists on gigantic subventions, will be strained. You have Russia, a state heavily dependent on oil, which will have to pipe down a little bit, and so on. There are huge implications if this is allowed to proceed. Obviously, there are huge roadblocks. The Keystone pipeline is an example, but there are lots of other roadblocks and people who do not want this to happen.

Sweeney: On the demand side of the market, we are exploring cars that do not use oil: electric vehicles, hybrid electrics, plug-in hybrids, battery electrics. Those will come in slowly. The hybrids have been in the market fifteen years now but only have a 3 percent market share. With battery progress, we could move to a point where the other major market for oil drops out at the bottom. So, then, with the geopolitical changes in the supply of natural gas and oil, then the major changes that could happen in switching between the energy forms that we have, it could be a whole new world. You have probably all heard before the statement that the Stone Age did not end because we ran out of stone. Neither will the oil age end because we have run out of oil. Well, that really can happen in my lifetime. Not just the lifetime of you students here, but in my lifetime. And we in North America are in the middle of that, and we have to make policy recognizing it. So, I fully agree with what Michael is saying there.

Wilson: You are also seeing a decline in consumption in the United States already.

Boskin: It will continue to decline, largely due to energy efficiency.

Sweeney: In 1974, when the Federal Energy Administration was started and they were debating the first corporate average fuel efficiency standards, the CAFE[5] standards, the average car on the road got twelve miles per gallon of gasoline. Now it gets over twenty-four. Going from twelve to twenty-four halves the amount of oil that you use per mile. The move to fifty-seven miles per gallon, matching the California standards, if possible at reasonable cost, would deeply reduce North American oil imports. Both domestic production and consumption are working right together.

Stephenson: Think about the Chinese in that context, both in terms of their needs, their horrible CO_2 emission problems, and their ability to access natural resources in Africa and, potentially, South America. What are they able to do to develop their own shale oil and gas resources? They have such resources; it is a question of how accessible they are. Do we help China with the technology to develop them? A big piece of what concerns us with China today has to do with how they are going to deal with energy from an internal standpoint.

Boskin: The Chinese are concerned about the global issues around CO_2 emissions. But their big problem is local pollution and its severe health consequences. These are much bigger political problems now and are causing protests among Chinese people. So they are going to have to do a lot of cleaning up. I do not think CO_2 emissions is the

---

5. Corporate average fuel economy.

main energy efficiency or environmental problem on their list. It may be highest on our list, because climate depends on global emissions. But they are dealing with their own local, horrible pollution problems.

O'Grady: Jaime, do you think that there is a national energy narrative, which is what Mexico needs at this point? And, specifically, is it true that the fiscal reform compensates for the loss of revenues? Wouldn't it be better to market the change in a more dynamic way, instead of scoring it statically, as if Mexico is going to lose? The expectation is that you are going to get a huge flow of new investment; between the royalties and all of the increased activity, the expectation is that in the end you are going to have more money. People are going to be better off in a variety of different ways. Government will have more; industry will have more capital; manufacturing will have access to cheaper energy; and Mexico will become more competitive. But that doesn't seem to be in the dialogue.

Serra Puche: You're absolutely right. There are two things that I am surprised are not in the dialogue. First, the potential growth effect and its consequences on the fiscal accounts. The second one is that Pemex is not only a monopoly, it's also a monopsony.[6] And the distortions that the monopsony has introduced are huge, because for a person to be a supplier or provider to Pemex, it's more important that you have connections. And therefore the lack of efficiency in the supply mechanism to the monopsony is very costly. When that changes and you have private companies buying all of the inputs that they need in the oil industry, then who you know is not going to be as relevant as how well you do it. It's not as relevant who you know as how well you know it. And I think that American firms are going to create a multiple effect on suppliers that are going to come into the industry. Eventually Pemex is going to have to resort to those suppliers as well.

The tax regime that Pemex has today is impossible. So if you want to have private firms with a normal tax regime, you're going to have to change the tax regime for Pemex as well, because it would be unfair

---

6. That is, Pemex is the sole purchaser of petroleum.

for Pemex to try to compete with Exxon if Exxon pays fewer taxes. The potential tax loss there is huge. So gradually they're going to have to adjust to all of this. And probably the effect on growth and development of the industry will come up with enough resources to compensate for that. But the decision to lower tax rates is before, not after. That's the complicated part.

Stephen Haber: The tax rate on Pemex is on gross value of production and is about the highest in the world. I think Syria may have a higher tax rate than Mexico. But Mexico is close. If you allow foreign companies in, you're going to have to give them a lower tax rate or they're not going to enter, and that's going to have a huge impact in the short run on government revenue.

Serra Puche: You know more about this than I, but the contracts are meant to be offered by the federal government, not by Pemex. So if I'm Exxon and I get a contract, then I'm competing with Pemex. If the tax regime I have is different from the one Pemex has, it's impossible for Pemex to compete. And it's also impossible to have the same regime that we have for Pemex. So the tax regime for Pemex is going to have to adjust.

O'Grady: The government is basically sucking all the earnings out of Pemex, and there is not enough reinvestment, so the output is going to plunge. Some might argue, "Look at all of this tax revenue we're losing." But in fact there's no way for the industry to survive on its current trajectory. And that just doesn't seem to be in the narrative.

There was an article in the *Wall Street Journal* last week that reported that environmental groups are trying to block permits for railcars within the US. One example was going from somewhere in the middle of the country to the West Coast. If they shut down pipelines and then there's more and more pressure on permitting for railroads, how are we going to get the oil?

Daniel Trefler: Canadian regulators have been trying to figure out what happened with the rail-to-rail modules. It's so explosive, US regulators were becoming concerned that the back-end oil is so volatile because of the extra gas that's inside of it. It's more dangerous to ship by rail. Canadians are very aware of it because US regulators are helping them. It's much more flammable. There's something in it that makes it much more flammable.

Boskin: While it is an important issue, different types of energy have very different flammability and combustibility thresholds. Gasoline is an order of magnitude less flammable and combustible than hydrogen, for example. Any type of energy has to deal with safety issues.

Dan and Lorenzo both, early on, emphasized these dynamic effects on innovation. There's been a starvation of reinvestment in Mexico, but also the technology frontier is so far beyond where Pemex is. Mexico has large potential reserves in the Gulf that aren't being exploited, so they need foreign firms that have that technology, to be able to access it reasonably and work safely, although there is a risk to everything. There's a lot of shale in a lot of places: Poland, Mexico, China. But in most of those places we really don't know how much is easily commercializable. It's not just building transport networks and pipelines, but also the rock formation and the geology. Fracking is not the same everywhere. Have there been any advances recently in studying that in Mexico that should be a high priority?

Serra Puche: People who are interested in shale think that the shale basin that is connected to Texas is exactly the same geology in Mexico as is being accessed in Texas. So the potential there is huge. Pemex has probably done some research, but they have not addressed the issue because they don't have enough money. We've been starving investment and CAPEX (capital expenditures) of Pemex over the last years. So there has been very little serious work.

Shultz: I think that North America has really arrived. But it is possible to mess it up. This Keystone decision could do it. At the last North American Forum meeting in Mexico City, the Canadian delegation there, who I thought were normally very sensible people, regarded it almost as an act of war, that there would be some retribution of some kind. It is not going to be taken lightly. And no doubt there are other things that could go wrong, but I think it is so promising a development, and there are such interesting developments that could make it work better, that it's really important to try to keep this together.

Wilson: But many people are looking at this as strictly business. It's not a question of emotions, saying the Americans are doing this or not doing that. They're just saying, do what you're going to do, but what you're going to do has consequences. We cannot leave a resource in the ground that is generating close to a hundred billion dollars a year of exports. So really the ball is in the US's court right now, to decide which way they want to go. But we must then take a business decision as to what the consequences are on this one project. As I said, we have two million barrels of oil still to come, and we don't have the capacity to move it all down here, so we're going to have to look at moving it elsewhere. Once those decisions are made, they will be based on long-term contracts; it's not something that you can just reverse. The pipeline companies will not get the financing unless they have contracts that they'll be able to carry for at least a significant part of the production.

Chapter Six

NAFTA's Next Twenty Years and Lessons for Future Trade Liberalization

The primary negotiators evaluate the advantages NAFTA has brought to North America and discuss how better rules for labor mobility would bring benefits, especially in light of changing demographics. They also examine trade pacts with Asia and Europe.

Presenters: Jaime Serra Puche, Michael H. Wilson, Carla A. Hills
Comments: Michael J. Boskin, George P. Shultz, Frank Montgomery Woods, Daniel Trefler, Stephen Haber, Alberto Diaz-Cayeros

Michael Boskin: We have discussed NAFTA's inception and negotiation, several different takes on evaluating its pros and cons, winners and losers, and how it helped modernize the Mexican economy and, to some extent, the Canadian economy. NAFTA's future, of course, occurs in the context of trade discussions, debates, and initiatives such as the Trans-Pacific Partnership (TPP) and the US-EU Transatlantic Trade and Investment Partnership (TTIP). What are some of the lessons from NAFTA for the future of trade liberalization? I refer specifically to these other trade agreements in the process of being negotiated, but also to other agreements that aren't working, or to NAFTA's future.

The proper economic way to think about trade liberalization is that the goal post is always moving. When trade isn't being liberalized, there is great temptation for special interest barriers and nontariff barriers and the like to grow like weeds. If you're not liberalizing and dealing with all of those things, gradually you recede, you fall back.

Jaime Serra Puche: I think the effects of NAFTA on Mexico provide a necessary perspective for thinking about the future of NAFTA. Trade liberalization, not only NAFTA, but trade liberalization in Mexico happened after we joined the GATT in 1986. It had a profound effect because we changed the relative prices between importable goods and exportable goods. Our closed economy had not been profitable. We had a distortion against exports in Mexico because we were protecting producers within the Mexican market. The Mexican producers were much more oriented to supplying the Mexican market than the foreign market, because they were making money through the protection margins. My regression of non-oil exports in Mexico on US GDP (when the American economy grows, we export more), against the effective tariff we charged to our imports, and against the exchange rate with the dollar, shows that the exchange rate is irrelevant in the long term. US GDP explains quite a bit, and a very good chunk of the growth of exports in Mexico is explained by the fact that we've lowered tariffs. The vertical axis in figure 6.1 is the effective average tariff Mexico charges to imports. The horizontal axis is the value of our non-oil exports. The lower the tariffs in Mexico, the more we were exporting. This is a very important lesson for a country like Mexico and other Latin American countries that haven't established the link between opening the economy and exporting more. They say, "When we lower tariffs, we're going to import more." But they don't go the extra step, showing that you export more. This is a very profound change in Mexico and it happened basically because of NAFTA. The main structural change in our export behavior occurred with NAFTA.

Figure 6.2 shows a very high correlation between Mexican GDP, particularly Mexican manufacturing production, and US GDP or US manufacturing production: it's almost one-to-one. Before NAFTA, the correlation was 0.21; after NAFTA the correlation index was 0.76, and econometric techniques reveal that this can be basically explained by NAFTA. There was another profound effect in Mexico, too. When Mexico was highly protected, people were producing for the domestic market and were only exporting residually. When we opened up, exports stopped being residual and became a true engine of growth.

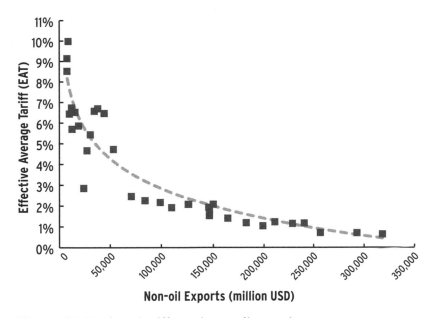

Figure 6.1 Mexican tariffs and non-oil exports.

Source: Data from US Bureau of Economic Analysis and Banco de México.

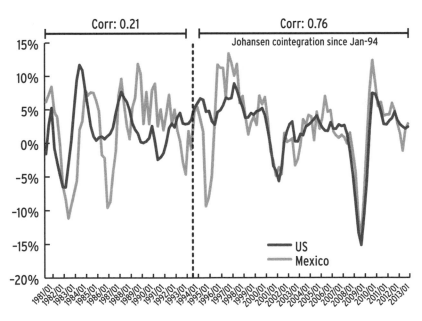

Figure 6.2 US industrial production and Mexico's manufacturing GDP, 1981: Q1-2013:Q1 (annual % change).

Source: Data from INEGI (Instituto Nacional de Estadística y Geografía) and US Federal Reserve.

Exports have been the most dynamic component of aggregate demand in Mexico since we introduced NAFTA. When we were closed, if Mexico started growing, exports would go down, because the Mexican market would take more products from Mexican producers and they were making more money selling in Mexico than abroad. At the same time, Mexico was importing more because we needed intermediate inputs. So whenever we started growing, we ended up with a balance-of-payments crisis because our exports would be going down and imports chronically going up. We would reach a deficit we could not finance; we went through traumatic periods like that time after time. This has changed. Now exports and imports correlate with each other and the trade balance in Mexico, which used to be a destabilization scheme, now is a stabilization mechanism.

Those two very profound changes had the following consequences. The first is that our exports have been growing dramatically. Figure 6.3 compares an index of world export growth and Mexican export growth since 1993, the year before NAFTA. The gap is increasing. Discounting the effect of world growth on exports, Mexico still made huge progress. The average Mexican exports more than the average Chinese, $2,600 per year versus $1,500. In fact, Mexico exports more per capita than every single BRIC[1] country.

George P. Shultz: But isn't it the case now that your labor costs are about the same? And your energy and transportation costs are less, so you're very competitive.

Serra Puche: In 1993, Mexico exported $144 million per day. Today Mexico exports more than $1 billion per day, which is almost a ten-times increase. Non-oil is $133 million against $883 million. The impact of those two changes is what I was referring to: relative prices of importables and exportables, and the coordination of the cycles, have resulted—among other things—in this huge growth of exports.

Before NAFTA, we were receiving $2.9 billion per year of foreign direct investment, FDI. That was the average between the period

---

1. Brazil, Russia, India, and China.

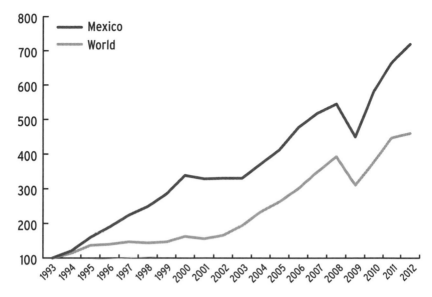

Figure 6.3 Non-oil exports (index 1993=100, 1993–2012).

Source: Data from INEGI (Instituto Nacional de Estadística y Geografía) and World Bank.

of 1980 and 1993 (figure 6.4). Now we're receiving almost $20 billion per year. That is the impact of those very dramatic changes in relative prices, coordination, and stability that NAFTA has helped produce.

Responding to George, a study by KPMG[2] has estimated how profitable each industry is in each country: autos, electronics, and so on. The Chinese are the most competitive. They have the largest profitability. The Indians are second. Mexico is third in the world. The US is number eleven and Canada is number nine, almost across all sectors. It means that Mexico is the most competitive country within NAFTA for manufacturing, according to these numbers. AlixPartners, a law and economics company, has looked at the cost of getting a product into the US market. In 2010, we were lower than the Chinese to get a product into the US and we're the number one competitive country to supply the US. When you add the numbers that George was mentioning, our relationship now with North America is much more

---

2. Auditing company.

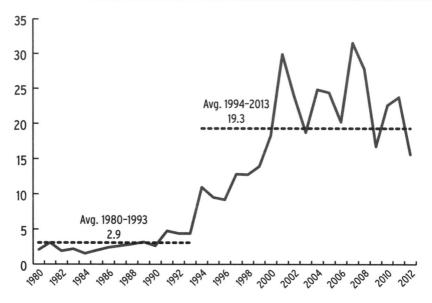

Figure 6.4 Foreign direct investment in Mexico (billion US dollars, 1993–2012).

Source: Data from INEGI (Instituto Nacional de Estadística y Geografía).

like production-sharing, compared to China, which is more a pure outsourcing mechanism.

Out of every dollar we export to the US, forty cents are American inputs; out of every dollar Canada exports to the US, twenty-five cents are American inputs. The average in NAFTA is thirty-two cents. So every single dollar that Canada and Mexico export to the US includes over thirty percent of American input. That has transformed the region. We're not just selling things to each other; now we're producing things jointly. Mexico contributes with certain levels of competitiveness for the following reasons. First, we have the cheapest gas in the world by far, and it will stay there for quite some time due to shale gas. We have an important and permanent advantage over Asian and European countries.

Our second competitive advantage is our demographics, as George mentioned. Figure 6.5 examines the NAFTA demographic pyramid. Adding the US, the Canadian, and the Mexican, you can see we have a dependency ratio that is much more sustainable over time than that of

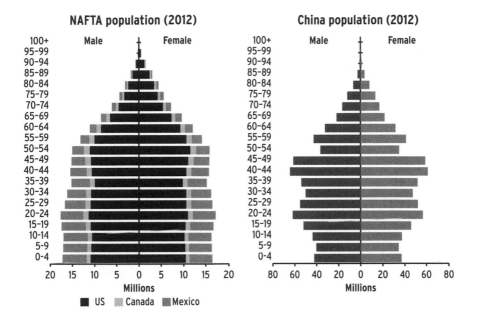

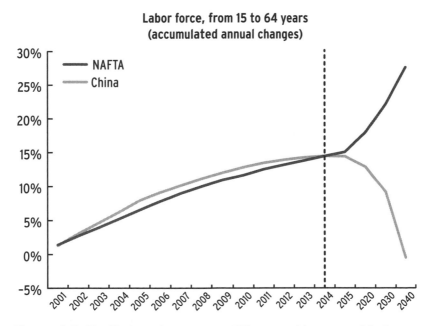

Figure 6.5 North American competitiveness (demographics).
Source: Data from US Census Bureau and National Bureau of Statistics of China.

the Chinese who, because of the one-child policy, will age very rapidly. The lower graph shows potential labor force projections, people ages fifteen to sixty-four. The North American line goes up; the Chinese line comes down, starting in 2015. We have an energy advantage, a labor advantage.

Shultz: China had a big decline in fertility, and for a while that was a dividend. They had an expanding labor force and a falling number of people the labor force had to support. That is now about to change, like throwing a switch. All of a sudden they're going to have a declining labor force and a rising number of people the labor force has to support. Furthermore, they've generated their productivity by moving people from rural areas to cities. The Chinese culture and history is that the safety net in China has been the family and the community. But people have been moved; they are more anonymous in cities. China is headed for some big problems. Mexico has the same demographics as China about twenty years later.

It's important for us in NAFTA to ask, "What do we do now to mitigate the impact of this switch that's going to take place?" It's baked in the cake; you know it's going to happen, so we should be working at it.

Serra Puche: The Chinese have just recently, I think, discussed or changed their one-child policy, right?

Shultz: Yes, but it's too late. This is happening. You can't change demographics just like that.

Carla A. Hills: Yes, and the policy change is limited: if one of the couple is a single child, then they may have a second child. So the change will not apply to everyone.

Serra Puche: Mexico will probably have very competitive labor for quite some time. Plus, if you look at transportation, we have an advantage between 12 and 15 percent over the Chinese to supply the American market, because of transportation costs and because we don't have to pay the MFN tariffs.

The transformation of Mexico has been enormous. We are the most competitive country supplying the US market and probably the Canadian market. We can contribute to the competitiveness of the area. And I think that there are three issues that we need to face intelligently. I agree with you about creating governance that is not bureaucratic. But there are issues that have to be solved. First is the architecture of NAFTA, which is going to change, regardless of what we do, because of the TPP and TTIP negotiations.

The TPP negotiation creates two potential problems for NAFTA. First, according to the Geneva Agreement, a new trade agreement dominates an older trade agreement. So if we end up with the three countries of NAFTA in the TPP negotiation, we could pretty much end up with the TPP substituting for NAFTA. From the American perspective, it's not the same when the Vietnamese export a microphone to the US with 4 percent of its value in inputs coming from the US, as it is importing it from Mexico and having 40 percent of the US value in its inputs. This is a different thing. Actually, most of the countries in TPP function as pure outsourcing to the US market, while Canada and Mexico are much more integrated to the US. So the rational thing to do, in my opinion, would be that all the products generated in North America should be ruled with the NAFTA rules. That has not been discussed. I don't see any true leadership thinking specifically about the consequences of TPP for NAFTA.

Hills: A majority of the countries that were negotiating within the TPP already have a free trade agreement with Mexico and also with the United States. So maybe the problem that you suggest is not as large, because we already give them free access.

Serra Puche: After the NAFTA negotiations on labor and environment, the US started incorporating all of the labor and environment rules into the text of its trade agreements, e.g., with Chile, and so on. These chapters are a part of the text and they jump into trade sanctions much more rapidly than in NAFTA. If Mexico were to lose these NAFTA rules and adopt the TPP rules, we could see a potential new instrument of protectionism growing in the US against Mexican exports. The other disadvantage is that they are not doing this with Fast Track. It's opening NAFTA to the cherry-picking in Congress, which I think is very dangerous.

Another architectural issue is the European issue. We already have a free trade agreement with Europe, the Canadians are almost finished with one, and the US is negotiating a free trade agreement. The natural thing would be to negotiate region-to-region. That would make sense for everybody, even for the Europeans. That would get rid of all of the spaghetti bowl of rules of origin. The USTR[3] has not reacted well to this proposal. Mike Froman thinks it is too complicated, and at this point I don't think it is possible anymore. However, there is a potential solution: a rule for convergence of the three agreements with Europe. After five years or so, make sure that the three separate agreements converge to one agreement. That will require some serious thinking, dialogue, and leadership, which I don't see so far.

An additional big issue for the future of NAFTA is labor mobility. If you make entry into the market difficult, you make exit from the market difficult. The economic agent that manages to enter does not want to leave the market. So the more difficult the US makes it for Mexicans to come to work in the US, the more difficult it is for them to go back to Mexico, because they don't want to lose the advantage and the opportunity of working in the US. Instead of just approaching labor mobility with a bill concentrated on the existing stock of Mexicans in the US, around 12 million people, which needs to be done, the bill should be complemented with some agreement on labor mobility that helps to take advantage of the demographics of the region and increases the competitiveness of the three countries.

Third, regarding the energy issue: I hope eventually we'll have more reasonable regulations in Mexico that will allow us, over time, to get an absolutely rational energy agreement in North America. That will give us a very important competitive advantage vis-à-vis the rest of the world.

Shultz: Let me raise a question on the labor mobility side. Given the demographics and the prospect of an improved Mexican economy,

---

3. United States Trade Representative.

shouldn't we expect a very small amount of immigration from Mexico to the US?

Serra Puche: The recent decline of Mexicans coming into the US is more explained by the slowdown of the American economy, particularly in construction, than by demographics. But you are right; eventually the demographics will go there. Your point is very important because, if the US decides to allow for a labor mobility scheme with the Canadians and Mexicans, the flows will not be as gigantic as they were in the past. That might facilitate things. The point here is that the current decrease in immigration is explained more by the decline of US construction than by the demographics. But, yes, in the long term the demographics will help.

Shultz: We have a big stake in getting better control of your (Mexico's) southern border. It's basically just an open border. The US-Mexico border is going to have a lot of non-Mexicans who constitute the illegal immigration problem. So we should focus on that.

Serra Puche: You're absolutely right; I agree. It's a tough one because of the geography of the border, the lack of institutions, and corruption. Our southern border is a disaster.

Boskin: Is there anything that America can do to assist with that?

Serra Puche: Yes. I think we have to sit down and talk about the NAFTA borders, not just the Mexico-US border. The immigration issue is not the US border with Mexico; it is the southern border of Mexico. We need to figure out how to do it intelligently, which is basically investment in infrastructure.

Hills: Long ago we had a program where Mexicans could come in. I think it was called the bracero program. And they could work and when the work was done go home to their families. We made it so difficult for them to go back and forth that now because of the scarcity of jobs they don't want to take the risk. I think that, in answer to

George's question, it is the lack of jobs, plus the danger and the difficulty of coming across a border where you can't get back and forth easily, that has really made the net immigration from Mexico zero today. It's hurting many sectors, particularly the agriculture sector, in our country.

Shultz: I don't think it's so difficult to get back, but you don't want to go back because it's so difficult to get back in again.

Frank Woods: From an agricultural standpoint, we're finding in Napa and Sonoma,[4] for all of the different crops that are grown on the north coast, that those who are citizens go back home for at least a month every year, some of them for two months. Their intent is not to retire in the United States but to retire permanently in Mexico. And we don't seem to recognize that.

Serra Puche: You are so right, Frank. They want to build a little house. They want to send a refrigerator to their mother. They want to buy a TV for their family. That's what they want to do. That's why they come here and work and get money. They would like to go back and improve the standard of living in Mexico, but we don't let them. The policy has been completely wrong.

Daniel Trefler: One of the big puzzles that we worry about in immigration is, why is each cohort of immigrants worse off than before? It's partly because there are two types of immigrants: those coming to live here forever and those who eventually intend to go back home. Actually, the cohort deteriorations are much less severe in Canada. That is a very important distinction about immigrant life in the US and in Canada.

Shultz: My impression is that people in Washington don't even grasp this conceptually. They don't even understand the problem.

---

4. Heavily agricultural counties in San Francisco Bay Area.

Trefler: Don't you think they understand it all too well, which is changing the political equilibrium once you change who is voting?

Shultz: No, I don't think that.

Boskin: I think that after this election, there will be an opportunity for immigration reform that would allow people here illegally, subject to certain conditions, to get a card that would let them stay legally. We could have a guest-worker program and expand the H-1B visas. This would enable them to go back and forth with a green card and offer a path to citizenship after fulfilling some requirements, but only after the people who have waited in line legally. Immigration reform has been dealt a big blow by the implosion of the rollout of the Affordable Care Act, as most Republicans won't trust the Obama administration's promise of border enforcement.

Shultz: The citizenship issue is not really the problem. A green card in a way is better. A large proportion of these people don't even want citizenship. They want to be able to go back and forth to Mexico.

Serra Puche: Canada's experience with visiting workers from Mexico going to Canada was good?

Michael H. Wilson: It has worked well, because there is a very specific requirement on the people who are receiving the seasonal workers to follow certain rules. If they don't follow the rules, they don't get the opportunity to do it again.

Trefler: We've reestablished a visa requirement for Mexicans because of refugee status seekers. The temporary workers program is under fire right now and will be scaled back. It's a very large program so even scaling it back is not disastrous.

Serra Puche: But it can work?

Trefler: Yes, it can.

Alberto Diaz-Cayeros: Yes. I was undersecretary for industrial development in Chihuahua State in northern Mexico, arguably one of the states who were most benefited by NAFTA. In a few years, Chihuahua created 250,000 industrial jobs, so that was the net result of the agreement. However, in the United States, SMEs—small and medium enterprises—are the main provider of jobs. Such is the case for Mexico, except for Chihuahua, which is the other way around: the big companies provide most of the jobs.

The maquiladora industry after twenty, thirty years in the country, has turned out to have only 3 percent of local integration. Mexican companies are only 3 percent integrated into supply chains of the maquiladora. And such is the fear also, by the way, in the Pemex and the supplier race for the oil industry.

Is there a way that the three countries could come together and assure that the benefits are going to be distributed in a more successful way?

Serra Puche: The maquiladora disappeared with NAFTA in the seventh year. The maquiladora doesn't exist anymore. I think that this program resulted in a very low content of Mexican inputs in Mexican exports to the US, which is less than 10 percent. The maquiladora program was introduced sometime in the late '60s or early '70s. But the government did not want to open the economy; they just wanted to open the border. So they created the maquiladora scheme, which basically meant that you would get a duty drawback. You would import something, transform it, and then send it back. And you would get back the tariff you paid when you imported it. The condition was that you did not sell the product in Mexico; you could not pass that benefit to the Mexican consumer. It was a crazy scheme. The traditional maquila exporters did not know anything about the Mexican consumers. They were not allowed to sell to Mexicans, and they didn't have an incentive to look for Mexican suppliers because they were getting the benefit of a zero tariff. So the culture of Mexican exports grew around the maquiladora program. I think time will take care of it, but if you're asking us to accelerate that process, it's hard to know how.

Stephen Haber: Mexico has a scarcity of credit for commercial purposes. The share of Mexican GDP that is private credit to private firms is at Honduran levels. Mexico has an extremely small banking system. It always has, except for the boom of 1991–94, and you know how that ended. It's not an ownership issue, because the banks are now all foreign-owned. So the fundamental problem is a property-rights problem of how to enforce contracts in a country in which judicial institutions are quite weak. Most small-medium manufacturers rely on bank credit for working capital, so the absence of bank credit for them is a big impediment, and I don't know if the problem can be solved trilaterally. That's a problem that Mexico is working on, but it's a very slow process.

Serra Puche: We have a program with a bank called Nafinsa[5] that provides guarantees for small and medium firms. So the commercial banks get support from the development bank in case the small and medium firm doesn't pay. But that is tiny compared to the needs. Also, government procurement is highly corrupted, so SMEs cannot grow on that. The energy issue is going to really open up options, but I don't think that too many small and medium firms are going to take them, because they are not prepared. So it's an issue to which it would be difficult to try to incorporate a solution in NAFTA or a NAFTA-plus.

Wilson: While a natural step might be to try to integrate TPP and the European negotiations into NAFTA, there doesn't seem to be the support or the enthusiasm from the USTR. If we could get started with just a dialogue among the three countries as to how it might occur, we might at least put the building blocks in place.

Hills: I would encourage you to push harder.

Wilson: Some work is going on right now, but further progress is possible. It's important that the North American region bring people

---

5. Nacional Financiera.

together. The more we talk about the range of issues, the more we start thinking as a region, particularly in the policymaking area.

The first issue is border management. There has been a strategic dialogue under way between the United States and both Mexico and Canada. Further progress is possible, perhaps more so on a bilateral basis now than we have had on a trilateral basis. We have a steering committee and Mexico has a committee as well. Addressing trade facilitation, cross-border activity: IBETs[6] and Shiprider[7] are two binational approaches. Also, they are looking at critical infrastructure and cybersecurity. We have harmonized inspection of air passenger traffic and baggage, and we're looking at newer approaches on border clearance. There's a border infrastructure investment plan that I think is important. There are similar things happening with Mexico.

The approach should be to move the management of the border away from the physical border, to avoid bottlenecks at the border. "Cleared once, accepted twice" means that, if something is cleared in Vancouver or Montreal or at an airport in Canada, it doesn't have to be cleared again going into the United States market. These are all pilot programs. One of the questions that we have in Canada is whether the US bureaucracy is going to accept these on a permanent basis and bring them to scale. There may be a possibility of bringing the Canada-US and Mexico-US discussions together and having more of a trilateral dialogue. I'd add talking more than we have about the southern border in Mexico to see what might be done there.

On regulatory reform, we have councils in both countries working on it; there is a high level of activity. President Obama has issued an executive order authorizing the identity and elimination of unnecessary regulatory differences. It's certainly something that should be pushed as hard as possible. There has been good progress here and I hope that can continue. The agreement between President Obama

---

6. Integrated border enforcement teams.

7. Canada-US Shiprider, officially known as Integrated Cross-border Maritime Law Enforcement Operations, allows the Royal Canadian Mounted Police and the US Coast Guard to cooperate in maritime law enforcement.

and Prime Minister Harper on border management is doing some good work quietly. We haven't had high-level announcements on it, but there is good progress underway. Future progress on regulatory reform should bring the two councils together and share best practices and see what we can do jointly. Clearly there's an opportunity to improve competitiveness, both on the manufacturing and on the retail side.

The third area is in energy and climate change. The ironic thing is that the presidents and the prime minister agreed on increasing North American energy trade. We commit our governments to work with all stakeholders to deepen such cooperation. We support coordinated efforts in everything but the Keystone XL pipeline. Further opportunities here are unconventional resources, infrastructure, energy efficiency, environmental awareness. There might well be room for a three-country discussion of the existing energy resources that we have, on a North American basis, to understand the nature of the decline of the resources. That could start to guide decision-making, particularly on the regulatory side. Again, high-level dialogue is important.

Pandemic disease: there has been a North American-wide plan on an avian pandemic influenza starting from SARS[8] a few years back. There was work done on preparedness and response capabilities. People were stopped at the border during the SARS epidemic and people have been working on developing the guiding principles. But future progress in prevention, mitigation, preparedness, and response, and also recovery, is desirable.

The final area is defense and security. Both Canada and the United States have been helping Mexico reduce criminal activity. That involves both training and information sharing. While we are farther away from the US-Mexico border, it's certainly something that we are concerned about, because we see signs of the activity creeping farther north. There has been helpful support with legal training. There is the Mérida Initiative between the US and Mexico. Further progress would deepen the bilateral commitment to fighting transnational crime, improve communication and collaboration among our three

---

8. Severe acute respiratory syndrome.

countries, and focus on the drug issue. Some progress has been made in high-level individuals being extradited to the United States.

In conclusion, it may be difficult getting the progress that we'd like to see on the trade side, but there are these other areas that we can work on. I've identified five areas as ways in which we can continue cooperating as a region and better understanding the benefits. Again, just to underscore what I said before, Canada and Mexico should push as hard as we can to avoid provisions, in either the TTIP or the TPP, which will undermine the strengths and the successes that we've had with NAFTA. We need to explore whether there are ways that we can integrate these two agreements with NAFTA.

Hills: If we want to build upon the NAFTA, we're going to have to take action and activate the business sector, the media, and tell them what the facts are. We can't just say we need high-level meetings. High-level meetings come because of pressure from behind. And I daresay that the great majority of our elected leaders, including our president, do not have a clue of all the benefits that the NAFTA has brought to us and what more it could bring to us in the future. It has created a market of $19 trillion[9] and 460 million consumers, and we want to double exports? Let's look at the market. The fact is that the activity between our three nations has simply exploded over the past two decades and could grow dramatically in the future. We need to talk about that.

Today Canada is our single largest export market. Mexico is our second-largest export market. Yes, the twenty-eight combined states of Europe are larger, but we sell more to Mexico than we sell to the BRICs: Brazil, Russia, India, and China. We sell more to Mexico than we sell to the rest of Latin America. We sell more to Mexico than we sell to France, Britain, Germany, and the Netherlands combined. Americans don't know that. Our elected leaders don't know it, and you want to double exports? There are some steps we could take close to home.

I despair when I hear, "Well, we can't do that because our leaders are not doing this." I think that we ought to take advantage of what

---

9. In current dollars; $17 trillion in constant 2005 dollars.

we've created and build on it. Could we improve upon the NAFTA? Yes, we could move on these areas that Michael has eloquently discussed, but they won't be dealt with unless we activate the leadership. I believe that we ought to fight for getting our North American partners into TTP and the TTIP. I believe that there are arguments we could make to the leadership about why they should be in and why it would be hugely in the United States' interest.

One is that it would strengthen the transatlantic arrangement by adding 150 million consumers and $3 trillion, giving the agreement more heft and more opportunity. Secondly, it would reduce the complexity that would occur if our two neighbors don't join, because Mexico has a trade agreement with Europe. Canada concluded one in October and it will undoubtedly come into force in the not-too-distant future. If our entrepreneurs, whether they be small or large, have to face three different trade rules of origin and border red tape, this is not going to be the kind of agreement that the United States wants.

Thirdly, having the three North American governments participate would provide an opportunity to enhance our regulatory coherence. You talk about efficient border management. We don't even have the same customs form. I can't go to Mexico and use the same customs form throughout North America. I am talking about one person. What about a truckload of goods? We have created structures that impede our building upon the benefits of the North American Free Trade Agreement. We need to get rid of them, but it's not going to happen by saying, "The leaders have to get together." The media, business, and the Hoover Institution have to sell it, and have to sell it hard. This is as difficult as getting Fast Track more than twenty years ago; maybe harder, because today our elected leaders are so polarized. But this could bring them together; it could be a terrific advantage for Mexico, for Canada, and for us.

And there's another reason that we should do this. It would facilitate President Peña's efforts to liberalize and transform the economy in Mexico, which is something the United States wants and would benefit from. He could do what President Salinas did. He could use it as an umbrella to protect him politically from complaints about

"Why are you doing this?" He would have a wonderful response: "It's because I am joining a mega-agreement. Can you imagine I'm joining an agreement that involves more than 40 percent of world trade and 50 percent of global GDP? Look at the advantages for Mexico. So, of course, we've got to liberalize telecommunications, energy, labor, and the like." This is an opportunity for the benefit not only of Mexico, but for all of North America. So as we move forward in the twenty-first century and we think, "What should the trade issues be?" we should identify the goals and really fight for them.

Appendix

*Letter from President
George H. W. Bush*

GEORGE BUSH

December 5, 2013

Greetings to the distinguished attendees and former colleagues gathered at the Hoover Institute at this high-powered conference commemorating the 20th anniversary of NAFTA. I am told your proceedings will include a rigorous evaluation of what that landmark treaty accomplished, so I will refrain from appealing to your "kinder and gentler" instincts! Let the chips fall where they may, as the saying goes.

NAFTA has stood the test of time and, as such, it is fitting that I salute the two leaders with whom I was proud to work on achieving it -- Brian Mulroney and Carlos Salinas. One thing was certain back then: we knew getting this deal done wouldn't be easy. On several occasions, Brian referred to the fact that his political support was down to the members of his immediate family, and I know how he felt.

But we stayed the course, because in the end we believed that economic reform would contribute to increased political stability and democracy in the Western Hemisphere. We believed that not only would trade benefit our neighbors, it would open new markets – new opportunities – for tens of millions of businesses and investors.

Perhaps that is why signing the NAFTA agreement was one of my proudest moments as President. I viewed the agreement as a palpable step forward to greater prosperity and stability across the region.

Closer to home, NAFTA would not have been possible without the early championing of trade liberalization with Mexico by Jim Baker and Mike Boskin; the superb job Carla Hills and Bob Mosbacher did in negotiating it in extremely complex circumstances; and my successor and friend President Clinton and his team who lobbied hard for Senate approval.

I have always believed in free trade based on clear, enforceable rules, but the case for it needs to be re-asserted and defended every generation. Special interests with a protectionist bent are powerful, and the reality is there are some losers as well as winners in trade liberalization. So marshaling the intellectual and political capital to advance free trade needs to be a bipartisan effort, which it usually has been since the establishment of the GATT at the end of WWII.

Enough from me. Congratulations on "NAFTA At Twenty: The Past, Present and Future of the North American Free Trade Agreement." I am sure it will be a great success.

All the best,

G. Bush

Conference Participants

PRESENTERS

Michael J. Boskin is the Tully M. Friedman Professor of Economics and senior fellow, Hoover Institution, Stanford University; and research associate, National Bureau of Economic Research. He has also taught at Harvard and Yale. As chairman of the President's Council of Economic Advisers from 1989 to 1993, he helped initiate NAFTA, introduce emissions trading for sulfur oxide in the Clean Air Act, resolve the Third World debt and the savings and loan financial crises, and place controls on government spending. Earlier, on candidate Ronald Reagan's Tax Policy Task Force, he helped develop the policies that substantially lowered marginal tax rates, indexed tax brackets for inflation, accelerated depreciation, and created IRAs and 401(k)s. He chaired the blue-ribbon Commission on the Consumer Price Index, whose report has helped government statistical agencies around the world improve measures of inflation, GDP, and productivity. He is the author of more than 150 books and articles on economic growth, tax and budget theory and policy, US saving and consumption patterns, and the implications of changing technology and demography on capital, labor, and product markets. Recipient of numerous professional awards and citations, he is proudest of Stanford's Distinguished Teaching Award.

Lorenzo Caliendo is an assistant professor of economics at Yale School of Management. His research on international trade focuses on understanding the trade and welfare effects of international trade policy, on how firms' organizational structures and productivity change when firms grow as a consequence of foreign trade competition, and on the macroeconomic effects of international trade on growth. He is also a faculty research fellow at the National Bureau of Economic Research and is on the research staff of the Cowles

Foundation for Research in Economics at Yale. He is affiliated with the Department of Economics and the Jackson Institute for Global Affairs at Yale University. He holds a PhD in economics from the University of Chicago.

Caroline Freund is senior fellow at the Peterson Institute for International Economics in Washington, DC, since May 2013. She was chief economist for the Middle East and North Africa at the World Bank from 2011 to 2013 and has held various positions in the research departments of the World Bank, the International Monetary Fund, and the Federal Reserve Board. Freund works primarily on economic growth and international trade and also writes on economic issues in the Middle East and North Africa. She has published numerous articles in economics journals, including *American Economic Review, Quarterly Journal of Economics, Review of Economics and Statistics,* and the *Journal of International Economics,* and has contributed to many edited volumes. Her work has also been cited in leading magazines and newspapers, including *Business Week, The Economist, Financial Times, Wall Street Journal,* and the *Washington Post.* She is on the editorial board of *World Bank Economic Review* and is a member of the Center for Economic Policy Research. She received a PhD in economics from Columbia University in 1997.

Stephen Haber is the Peter and Helen Bing Senior Fellow at the Hoover Institution and the A. A. and Jeanne Welch Milligan Professor at Stanford University. He is a professor of political science, of history, and of economics (by courtesy), as well as a senior fellow of the Stanford Institute for Economic Policy Research and the Stanford Center for International Development. He is director of the Hoover Institution's Working Group on Intellectual Property, Innovation, and Prosperity. Haber investigates the political institutions and economic policies that delay innovation and improvements in living standards. Much of that work has focused on Mexico. He has authored or co-authored four books and dozens of scholarly articles on the Mexican economy and is a corresponding member of Mexico's National

Academy of Science. His most recent book, co-authored with Charles Calomiris, is *Fragile by Design: The Political Origins of Banking Crises and Scarce Credit* (Princeton University Press, 2014). It examines how governments and industry incumbents often craft banking regulatory policies in ways that stifle competition and increase systemic risk.

Carla A. Hills is chairman and chief executive officer of Hills & Company International Consultants, which provides advice to international firms on investment, trade, and risk assessment issues, particularly in emerging market economies. She served in the cabinets of President George H. W. Bush as US Trade Representative and of President Gerald R. Ford as secretary of the Department of Housing and Urban Development. She also served as an assistant attorney general in the Civil Division of the Department of Justice in the Ford administration. She serves on the international advisory board of J. P. Morgan Chase and is a member of the board of Gilead Sciences. She serves on many not-for-profit boards and is co-chair of the Council on Foreign Relations, Inter-American Dialogue, and International Advisory Board of the Center for Strategic and International Studies. She chairs the National Committee on US-China Relations and is a member of the Executive Committee of the Peterson Institute for International Economics and of the Trilateral Commission. She is a member of the secretary of state's Foreign Affairs Policy Board.

Mickey Kantor, a lawyer with Mayer Brown, concentrates his practice on corporate and financial international transactions. He has extensive experience in market access issues as well as the expansion of client activities in foreign markets through trade, direct investment, joint ventures, and strategic business alliances. Before joining Mayer Brown, he was secretary of commerce (1996–97) and US Trade Representative (1993–96). He was recently recognized in *The International Who's Who of Business Lawyers—Trade & Customs 2009*. Among his awards and honors: the Civic Medal of Honor by the Los Angeles Area Chamber of Commerce, the Order of the Southern Cross Award by the government of Brazil (2001), the William O. Douglas

Award by the Constitutional Rights Foundation, the Thomas Jefferson Distinguished Public Service Medal from the Center for the Study of the Presidency, the Albert Schweitzer Leadership Award from the Hugh O'Brien Youth Foundation, and the Elihu Root Distinguished Lecturer, Council on Foreign Relations. Kantor chairs the Pacific Council on International Policy, Los Angeles 2020 Commission, and Center for Communication Leadership and Policy.

Jaime Serra Puche is chairman of SAI Law and Economics (consulting firm) and founder of Aklara (electronic auctions), CAM (Arbitration Center of Mexico), and the NAFTA Fund of Mexico (private equity fund). He worked in the Mexican government from 1986 to 1994 as undersecretary of finance, secretary of trade and industry, and secretary of finance. As secretary of trade and industry, he led the negotiation and implementation of NAFTA; headed the negotiations of free trade agreements with Chile, Colombia, Venezuela, Bolivia, and Costa Rica; and promoted the creation of the Federal Competition Commission in Mexico. His not-for profit boards include the Corporation of Yale University (1994–2001), where he co-chaired the President's Council on International Activities. He is a trustee of the National Institute for Genomic Medicine in Mexico and of the Trilateral Commission. Serra Puche is a director of the board of the following publicly listed companies in the NYSE: The Mexico Fund (MXF), Tenaris (TS), and Grupo Modelo (GMODELOC).

George P. Shultz is a native of New York. He graduated from Princeton University in 1942. After serving in the Marine Corps, he earned a PhD at MIT. Shultz taught at MIT and the University of Chicago Graduate School of Business, where he became dean in 1962. He was appointed secretary of labor in 1969, director of the Office of Management and Budget in 1970, and secretary of the Treasury in 1972. From 1974 to 1982, he was president of Bechtel Group Inc. Shultz served in the Reagan administration as chairman of the President's Economic Policy Advisory Board (1981–82) and secretary of state (1982–89). He is honorary chairman of the Stanford Institute for Economic Policy Research and chairs the Shultz-Stephenson Task Force on Energy Policy at the Hoover Institution, the Precourt Institute for Energy Efficiency Advisory Council at Stanford University, and the MIT Energy Initiative External Advisory Board. Since 1989, he has been a Distinguished Fellow at the Hoover Institution.

James L. Sweeney is director of the Precourt Energy Efficiency Center and professor of management science and engineering at Stanford University. His professional activities focus on economic policy and analysis, particularly in energy, natural resources, and the environment. He currently is a senior fellow of: the Stanford Institute for Economic Policy Research; Hoover Institution; Freeman Spogli Institute for International Studies; and Precourt Institute for Energy. Sweeney is a senior fellow of the US Association for Energy Economics, a council member and senior fellow of the California Council on Science and Technology, and a member of the External Advisory Council of the National Renewable Energy Laboratory. He earned his bachelor's degree from MIT in electrical engineering and his doctorate from Stanford University in engineering-economic systems.

Daniel Trefler is the J. Douglas and Ruth Grant Canada Research Chair in Competitiveness and Prosperity and professor of economics in the Rotman School of Management, University of Toronto. He holds degrees in economics from the University of Toronto (BA), Cambridge University (MPhil), and UCLA (PhD) and is affiliated with the Canadian Institute for Advanced Research and the National Bureau of Economic Research. He is co-editor of the *Journal of International Economics* and the *Journal of Economic Literature*. Awards include the Canadian Economics Association's Innis Award "in recognition of contributions to economics in the broad sense" and the McDonald Award for contributions to early childhood research and advocacy. He is a member of the Ontario Government's Task Force on Competitiveness and the C. D. Howe's International Economic Policy Council. He oversaw the economic research that backstopped the Comprehensive Economic and Trade Agreement

(CETA) negotiations. He studies the impact of international trade on innovation, employment, earnings, and domestic institutions. His current research focuses on domestic and international levers for promoting competitiveness and broad-based prosperity.

Michael H. Wilson is chairman of Barclays Capital Canada Inc. and is currently responsible for managing Barclays Capital's client relationships in Canada. He was Canada's ambassador to the United States from 2006 to 2009. Before that, he was chairman of UBS Canada and, in 2001, a vice chairman of RBC Dominion Securities. Wilson served in the House of Commons from 1979 until 1993. In 1984, he was appointed minister of finance until 1991. He then became minister of industry, science, and technology and minister for international trade. He has been active in a number of professional and community organizations, including Brain Canada and Centre for Addiction and Mental Health. He is currently chancellor of the University of Toronto and chairs the Governing Council of the Canadian Institutes of Health Research. He is a Companion of the Order of Canada and has honorary degrees from the University of Toronto, York University, Trinity College at the University of Toronto, and the Royal Military College of Canada.

COMMENTERS

Kyle Bagwell is the Donald L. Lucas Endowed Professor in Economics at Stanford University. He is also a senior fellow of the Stanford Center for International Development and a research associate at the National Bureau of Economic Research. Bagwell received his BA from Southern Methodist University in 1983 and his PhD from Stanford University in 1986. Before Stanford, he taught at Northwestern University and Columbia University. He served as a reporter for the American Law Institute Project on Principles of Trade Law: The World Trade Organization. He is a fellow of the Econometric Society. His research has been published in numerous professional journals. He is the co-author of *The Economics of the World Trading*

System with Robert W. Staiger (Cambridge, MA: The MIT Press, 2002).

Alberto Diaz-Cayeros is former undersecretary for industrial development for Chihuahua state, Mexico.

Brian Lippey is the founder and CEO of Caledonian Partners LLC, a diversified investment company headquartered in Greenwich, Connecticut, that advises and raises capital for alternative asset managers.

Mary O'Grady, a journalist at the *Wall Street Journal,* writes "The Americas," a weekly column on politics, economics, and business in Latin America and Canada.

Diego Perez is a doctoral candidate in economics at Stanford University.

Thomas F. Stephenson has been a partner at Sequoia Capital, a leading Silicon Valley-based venture capital firm, since 1988. He previously spent twenty-two years with Fidelity Investments. During the latter part of the George W. Bush administration and the early months of the Obama administration, he served as US ambassador to Portugal. A Harvard graduate (BA, MBA), he is a member of that university's board of overseers. He is vice chairman of the Hoover Institution's board of overseers and and co-chairs the Shultz-Stephenson Energy Task Force.

Alan Sykes is Robert A. Kindler Professor of Law, New York University Law School, and a leading expert on the application of economics to legal problems.

John B. Taylor is the Mary and Robert Raymond Professor of Economics at Stanford University; George P. Shultz Senior Fellow in Economics at the Hoover Institution; and director of Stanford's

Introductory Economics Center. He is known for his economic research on the foundations of monetary theory and policy. He served as a member of the President's Council of Economic Advisers (1989–91) and undersecretary of treasury for international affairs (2001–05). Recipient of numerous awards, he won the 2012 Hayek Prize for his latest book, *First Principles: Five Keys to Restoring America's Prosperity*.

Frank Montgomery Woods is the founder and president of Clos du Bois Wines in Sonoma County. He is a Hoover Council member.

Index